# The Power of Ren
## of Ren
### China's Coaching Phenomenon

# The Power of Ren

## China's Coaching Phenomenon

Eva Wong
and
Lawrence Leung

John Wiley & Sons (Asia) Pte Ltd

Published in 2007 by John Wiley & Sons (Asia) Pte Ltd
2 Clementi Loop, #02-01, Singapore 129809

This Publication is designed to provide accurate and authoritative information
with regard to the subject matter covered. It is sold with the understanding that
the Publisher is not engaged in rendering professional services. If professional
advice or other expert assistance is required, the services of a competent
professional person should be sought.

*Other Wiley Editorial Offices*

John Wiley & Sons, Inc., 111 River Street, Hoboken, NJ 07030, USA
John Wiley & Sons Ltd, The Atrium Southern Gate, Chichester P019 8SQ,
    England
John Wiley & Sons (Canada) Ltd, 5353 Dundas Street West, Suite 400, Toronto,
    Ontario, M9B 6HB, Canada
John Wiley & Sons Australia Ltd, 42 McDougall Street, Milton, Queensland 4064,
    Australia
Wiley-VCH, Boschstrasse 12, D-69469 Weinheim, Germany

*Library of Congress Cataloging-in-Publication Data*

ISBN-13: 978-0-470-82215-9
ISBN-10: 0-470-82215-5


Typeset in Chaparral, points 10.5 by Hot Fusion
Printed in Singapore by Saik Wah Press Pte Ltd

10 9 8 7 6 5 4 3 2 1

# Contents

Introduction ................................................................... vii

**Part 1** 🔲 **People, Not Issues**

1     The Human Touch ........................................... 3

**Part 2** 🔲 *Ren* **at Work**

2     Changing Attitudes ............................................ 41

3     Finding Opportunities in Crisis ....................... 51

4     From Chaos to Prosperity ................................. 67

5     Revolutionizing Retailing ................................. 83

6     From Management to Leadership ..................... 99

7     Going to the Mountain ...................................... 115

8     Living out a Prophesy ........................................ 131

9     Believing in Coaching ....................................... 145

10    From Rags to Riches .......................................... 155

**Part 3** 🔲 **The** *Tao* **of** *Ren*: **Nine-Dot Leadership**

11    Making Dreams a Reality ................................... 171

Postscript by Lawrence Leung ....................................... 273

Index ............................................................................... 281

# Introduction

Sometimes a solitary word or a single question can send your life on a journey you had never imagined.

In 1986, while working for the Canadian Embassy's South China Trade Office in Hong Kong, I led a delegation of Canadian business-people to Guangzhou, the provincial capital of Guangdong province. Guangzhou is just two hours from Hong Kong by train, but in those days it might well have been on the other side of the world. Hong Kong was still a British-administered colony, and China was literally another country. The city I called home was an outpost of free trade, Western fashions, and cosmopolitan culture. As for many other Hong Kong nationals, China was "that place over the border."

Hong Kong, of course, is a city of immigrants, the overwhelming majority of them from that place over the border. My parents numbered among them. My father hailed from rural Fujian, and my mother was born in Shanghai in the giddy days when the city was feted as the Paris of the East. Like many Chinese who made Hong Kong their home, in 1949 she escaped when the Chinese Revolution marched into town and pulled the switch on Shanghai's bright lights. She was just 24 at the time, and her life during those years before she made Hong Kong her home is mostly a blank for me. All I know is that she was orphaned at the age of four and brought up by her father's parents.

If my parents' China years were a blank page for me, then so was China when I made that first visit. After a lifetime in Hong Kong, going to Guangzhou seemed like a journey into an alternative history. The city was drab and gray. Where I came from, the upwardly mobile aspired to own a BMW, or a similarly prestigious imported car – as much status symbol as vehicle. But in Guangzhou there were very few cars on the roads. The local population, dressed in uniform button-down Mao suits, navigated the cluttered streets on legions of clunky, Chinese-made bicycles. I remember thinking, *Where are the traffic lights?* On my first day, it was difficult for me even to summon up the courage to cross the road.

I was only dimly aware of the fact at the time, but I had arrived in China at yet another pivotal point in the country's modern history. Mao Zedong's revolution of 1949 had put an end to the turmoil of a long-fought civil war with the Nationalists, or Kuomintang – who were forced into flight to Taiwan. But peace came at a cost. Preoccupied with shoring up the borders of its sprawling territories, and with consolidating the central authority of the Chinese Communist Party, China became a hermit nation for the next three decades.

With the death of Mao in 1976, and the rise of Deng Xiaoping, change was in the air. In 1978, Deng announced a new "open-door" policy, ushering in the establishment of two "special economic zones" just over the border from Hong Kong and from Macau – Hong Kong's sister colony, at the time administered by Portugal. The earliest investors were "compatriots" from Hong Kong and from the Nationalist enclave of Taiwan, but others soon joined the rush. By the time I arrived in Guangzhou, China fever was building and the country was emerging as the world's fastest-growing economy.

These were all somewhat abstract developments for me. I knew that China was changing, but I saw this mostly in a negative light. There was a pun doing the rounds at the time, a play on an old Communist Party slogan that exhorted the people to "Look to the future!" Although they are written differently, in Mandarin Chinese – or *Putonghua*, "the common tongue" – "future" is pronounced identically to "money." And so, "Look to the money!" was the catch-cry of the latest new China, people joked.

It is difficult to convey the feeling this play on words had for people like myself from affluent, modern Hong Kong, but it evoked what many of us at the time saw as the grasping, hardscrabble world across the border. People there had dreams, we knew, but they were so far away, so impossible to realize. And, besides, what did it all have to do with me, anyway? I had a comfortable job at the Canadian Embassy, a family, a blessed life in one of the world's most prosperous capitalist enclaves. True, in 11 years time Hong Kong would yield its sovereignty from Britain to China and in theory the border that separated us from our less fortunate neighbors would cease to exist. But that was an age away. Who knows, perhaps, like many other Hong Kong people, I would emigrate to Canada when the time came.

These were the kinds of thoughts that swam in my head during that trip – until one of the members of the delegation I was leading asked me a very innocent question.

"Where are you from?"

I suppose the questioner had overheard me speaking Cantonese – the southern Chinese dialect shared by Hong Kong and most of

Guangdong province – and had wondered whether I was a local.

The question caught me off guard, and without thinking, I replied: "Hong Kong."

The words tumbled out of my mouth. But as they did, I experienced what I can only describe as a kind of electric shock. Where *did* I come from? What did I mean when I said I was from Hong Kong? I realized there wasn't even a word to describe the nationality I had just used to describe myself. It is easy enough to say you are American, or British, or Japanese, but me ... what should I say? I'm a Hong Konger? Hongkongese?

It took me some time to think it through – and even longer to do something about it – but the answer I now give when someone asks me where I am from is: "I'm Chinese."

*The Power of Ren* is not a book about my personal journey, even if I cannot help but wonder whether it would have been written if that question, "Where are you from?" had not thrown me into such confusion in Guangzhou in 1986. Rather, *The Power of Ren* is a contribution to the ongoing story that is usually filed under "the rise of China." But, unlike most of the other books on this subject, with their emphasis on export earnings, annual per-capita gross domestic product, political analysis, and geopolitical implications, it is a book about the transformation of people. And this book begins with my transformation.

For me, the question, "Where are you from?" sparked a hundred more questions. It made me wonder where I belonged, what I was doing with my life, whether I was fulfilling my potential. It led me away from a marriage I had felt stifled in, into advanced studies in the United States and Canada, and back to China to be part of the latest revolution in the country I now recognize as home. I had the remarkable good fortune to be exposed to ideas that have long been transforming the way people do business and realize their dreams in the West, and they were ideas that changed my life. But, as I underwent this transformation, I realized that it had come about largely because of the privileged circumstances of my life.

As a Hong Kong Chinese, I have had opportunities that are open to very few of China's 1.3 billion people. In theory, China has been "rising" since Deng Xiaoping announced his "open-door" policy in 1978, but the reality is that it is only in the past 15 years that China's entrepreneurial revolution has taken place. For the vast majority of urban Chinese, life is still a frantic game of catch-up, and very few of them have the time – let alone the skills that are now widely available in the West – to give any thought to whether they are using their skills to their best potential, working as effectively as they might, or – as I am doing now – fulfilling their dreams.

It was this that brought me back to China. If I had learned nothing else from my advanced studies and practical experience in Hong Kong after I returned from overseas, it was that there was enormous potential for China to benefit from the lessons of corporate coaching. I began to think about ways that modern Western concepts of self-actualization and coaching could be introduced into a Chinese environment and not sound like an artificially imported philosophy from the West. In actual fact, the more I thought about it, the easier I realized it was. All the ideas I had been exposed to on my personal journey already existed in the Chinese tradition. It was just a matter of reminding my Chinese audience of their own history.

*The Power of Ren* is the story of those ideas, some of the people whose lives they have touched, and how they are now making more effective contributions to the fastest growing economy in the world.

***Eva Wong***

PART 1

# PEOPLE,
## NOT ISSUES

# Chapter 1

# The
# HUMAN
# TOUCH

Close on 200 clients are assembled in the convention hall of a four-star hotel in southern China. Perhaps half of them are from Guangzhou, the nearby capital of Guangdong province, which borders Hong Kong. But the rest come from all over China – from the mountainous southwestern province of Sichuan, from far northern Heilongjiang, and even from as far away as Urumqi, the capital of Xinjiang province. It is day two of a four-day course, and everyone present has been through an intense program of experiential exercises that are challenging their notions of who they are and how they carry out their relationships with others.

A trainer is on the stage. In Cantonese-accented Mandarin he explains the rules of the Red and Black Game. For the Red and Black Game, he says, everyone in the room will separate into two, nearly 100-strong groups. Each group will retire to a different room, where they will have half an hour to cast six votes either for red or for black. On a large piece of white paper hung on an easel, a training assistant writes the scoring method for the game. If both teams vote black, each receives a positive score of three. If one team votes red and the other votes black, the team that votes red receives a positive score of five and the team that votes black receives a negative score of five. If both teams vote red, each receives a negative score of three.

"In order for a vote to be valid," the trainer says pointedly, "everyone has to vote. The purpose of the game is to win, and the way to win is to accumulate the maximum positive scores."

Pandemonium erupts the moment the two groups are separated and are faced with the task of voting for a color. For a start, there are immediate organizational challenges, as 100 people who have never worked together as a team before are suddenly confronted with the challenge of putting a voting system in place. Meanwhile, as a handful of people struggle to take charge, others are arguing strategy, and there seems to be as many theories on which color the team should vote for as there are people in each of the two rooms. There are also competing theories about the objective of the game. Is it simply an organizational challenge – to get six votes carried out in such a short space of time – or is there some other point to the game?

But as a kind of a calm descends on the room, and several self-appointed leaders manage to get the group to vote by taking seats on either side of the room – red votes on one side, black on the other – a fragile consensus begins to emerge on both sides that voting black amounts to suicide if the other team votes red. And as the minutes tick by, one team manages to cast five votes for red and the other three votes for red.

When the teams are reassembled together in the convention hall, the trainer again takes to the stage. One by one he has clients in the audience stand up and explain which team they thought won, and why. Invariably, the answer is that Team A won because it managed to cast more votes than Team B. The spirit of the questioning is almost an interrogation, and client after client is asked how their team could have won if they ran up a negative score by voting red every time. Abruptly the coach switches gears and tells the audience a story.

In Canada, on one occasion, he says, two teams played the Red and Black Game for far longer than the half-hour those in the room had just been playing it. In fact, they played it for close on 24 hours, in the hope that a winner would emerge. For hour after hour, Team A sent out a red ticket, and Team B sent one back. Despite the fact that exhaustion began to set in as time went by, just one person – an elderly woman on Team A – began to protest. "This is ridiculous," she said in frustration. "If we just send out red tickets, and they send red tickets back, no one can win this game." But her teammates argued back that if they relented and started sending out black tickets, the other team would probably just continue sending out red tickets and start to get ahead. And so the team continued on with its red-ticket strategy.

They continued for several more hours, sending red tickets out and getting red tickets back. Until the elderly woman again began to protest. For some hours she had been sitting and watching the game unfold, and she began to think about her family history – with its heartbreaks and feuding silences, rows, and separations. Suddenly she realized the game was an analogy, a mirror on life, and she saw that all her life she had been sending out red tickets and getting red tickets back. As a wife and a mother for much of her life she had played the role of a victim, never allowing herself the right to stand up and make a difference, but here in the Red and Black Game she realized she could make a difference, not only by speaking her mind, but also – ultimately – by withholding her vote. Not only that, she saw that the way her team was playing the game was very much like the way people play life – hurting themselves and those around them. It was a revelation. Profoundly moved, she got to her feet in tears and told the team what she had realized. This time, she said, she would refuse to cast her vote unless the team understood what kind of game it was playing, and changed the way it was playing it in order to achieve a win-win outcome. It was a turning point. Moved by what they had heard, Team A sent out – after nearly a day and a night – its first black ticket. Sure enough, Team B sent back a red ticket. But the mood had changed on Team A, and after sending out that first black ticket, a consensus quickly emerged that the only way forward was to continue sending out black tickets. For another hour, every time Team A sent out a black ticket, Team B sent back a red one. Until finally Team B, for the first time, reciprocated with a black ticket of its own.

"The two teams," the trainer explains, "had finally turned a losing situation into a win-win situation." Pressing his point home to an audience that is listening with rapt attention, the trainer continues. "Here we are in southern China. And what's going on here? All those Chinese companies just up the road from here who are exporting electronics and computer peripherals to the international market – what are they doing? They're undercutting each other, putting each other out of business, hurting themselves, in order to try and get ahead in a cut-throat market. They're engaging in price wars which no one can win, rather than trying to find ways to cooperate for their mutual benefit. They're throwing out red cards when they could be throwing out black ones – fighting among each other when they could be working together."

##  COACHING FOR CHANGE

The scene described is from the *Ren* Coaching Model®'s program. It is one of many situations we put clients through in China to start them looking at themselves and their relationships differently. The method for doing this is called coaching. This is a relatively new profession, and while it has made some headway in North America, in China it is only just starting to have an impact on the way people do business and interact with each other.

In China, when people first hear about coaching, they assume it must be some kind of training. But coaching and training are very different. Training is the transference of skills. If we don't know how to use certain computer software, then someone can teach us the skills that we need. But coaching comes into play when we *think* we are not smart enough to learn to use certain computer software – when we have a problematic perception of ourselves that is holding us back. When coaches confront a situation like this, they help us to clarify our goals, uncover the truth about what is holding us back, shift that interfering mindset, and then set our goals. And they do that simply by listening, asking questions, making distinctions, and giving feedback.

Of course, there are elements of training in what we do in China – at the end of the day, we are training people to be coaches themselves. And the Red and Black Game, after all, is a training exercise that gives people an experiential understanding of a key concept in the *Ren* Coaching Model repertoire. But guiding the proceedings is the coaching technique: listening, asking questions, making distinctions and providing feedback. Coaching, in short, is about people, and about providing an environment in which they can achieve their goals through a more effective attitude.

 ## THE HUMAN TOUCH

## PUTTING PEOPLE FIRST

During a discussion about the importance of putting people first in an organization, one of our coaches described a movie she had seen. The lead character was an idealistic young doctor, and in one scene he finds himself attending a lecture given by a senior doctor. In the presence of an actual patient suffering from a rare disease, the doctor begins to give a scientific explanation of the patient's symptoms and the various ways they might worsen if they are not treated correctly. He is so rapt up in his lecture that he doesn't notice that the patient is listening with a look of mounting horror and dismay.

Finally, exasperated, the young doctor interrupts the lecturer, and asks him whether the patient he is talking about has a name. The lecturer stops in surprise and looks at the patient, who breathes a sigh of relief at being recognized as a living human being and not just a medical specimen.

All of us can forget at times that we are surrounded by living, breathing human beings who have feelings just like our own. While it is important to be professional and focused on results, we also have to remember that getting results requires us to work together with other people.

People are not objects or serial numbers. Coaching makes a difference because it returns us to our relationship with ourselves and others, transforming the organization we are a part of into a place that is focused on people, not on issues.

When we look at a problem in the workplace, we have a tendency to overlook the people. It is not our fault, really; it is the way Western thought has evolved over thousands of years. There must be a reason why things are the way they are, and it is our job to find out what that reason is, we say to ourselves – and, if we are a consultant, to anyone who will pay to listen. This is the way we have been taught to think by generations of great minds, from Plato to Freud, right on down to the likes of Edward de Bono and Jack Welch. If we can just find out what is causing a certain problem, we can fix it and everything will be back to normal.

Of course, the average manager is not unaware that people are part of any management problem. But conditioning and training conspire to make them downplay the importance of people. Who has not attended a business meeting and heard the phrase, "Focus on the issue, not on the person"?

In other words, forget about *who* is at the center of the problem, and look only for clues as to *what* the problem is. Put aside our feelings about the personal relationships that are at the heart of the problem, and focus on the external factors that are causing it.

To be fair, this is often an effective approach to problem-solving, whether in a company or in a relationship. Solutions are found without upsetting the balance of the personal relationships involved, and the matter is resolved with the least possible impact on the harmony of the group. "Issues, not people" company meetings can be run along structured lines, and everyone involved is encouraged not to take things personally. At their best, such meetings result in a team or an individual arriving at new methods that fix whatever was broken, and the problem is solved.

 OR IS IT?

After a decade of corporate coaching in China, we have seen enough of "issues, not people" management theory to believe it is not a solution – and particularly in China. In a society that is so fundamentally centered on relationships, where the family unit is the nucleus of a complex web of social interaction that has underpinned civilization for thousands of years, a purely objective approach to problem-solving simply does not create sustainable solutions. Central to many of the problems in Chinese companies is people's behavior, and we cannot expect a person's behavior to change unless they *choose* to change it. Without that choice being made, all that is possible is a temporary reprieve.

## THE "ISSUES, NOT PEOPLE" EXCUSE

A coach was talking to a group of clients taking a *Ren* Coaching course. He pointed out that often when managers tell their staff that they are issues-focused rather than people-focused, they are not being entirely honest. "Usually, when a manager says something like that, what they're actually saying is, 'I don't know how to inspire you.' Making out that they are issues-oriented is actually a form of escape. In this context, being focused on issues, not people, is an excuse.

Coaching is not all about this *thing*, but about this *person*. When we wake up to ourselves and break through our self-imposed boundaries, *things* are no longer problems that cannot be resolved. So, coaches often ask clients: "What is it you need to change about yourself in order to get results?"

A client might say in response, "In order to get things done properly, I need to make some personnel changes."

"Of course, you can make personnel changes," the coach is likely to reply, "if that's really going to help you reach your objectives. But how about, while you're making those changes, you also try and inspire those people you want to get rid of to learn and improve? If you don't, it's likely that every time you encounter problems, your only solution will be to make personnel changes."

As a manager, it is only when we can inspire the *people* around us to improve, that *things* will really start to improve.

But it goes further than that. When we step back, we often find that objective analysis causes more problems than it solves. The immediate problem may have been resolved, but inevitably another process is set in motion – a process that in its turn grinds out another problem once the conditions are right.

Why does this happen? Someone paying for a consultation might say that it is because management consultants need to create more work for themselves. But the truth is usually more innocent. In fact, it is the logical approach that is to blame. Too often, addressing problems logically leaves the people at the heart of them unchanged.

This impersonal way of dealing with problems seldom works in China, where an "issues, not people" approach to colleagues and subordinates is unlikely to meet with success. The Chinese equivalent of, say, Jack Welch could never call up a subordinate (as Welch's successor as CEO of General Electric, Jeffrey Immeldt, recalled in an interview in 2005), and say to him: "You know I love you, but your division has a problem, and you had better fix it or I will fix you." In Chinese society, *everything* is personal. What the subordinate would have expected is a chat over a cup of tea, where the discussion would be centered on family, friends, and other interests – and for the message to be delivered in the most subtle of ways.

All the same, China is changing. International management studies are becoming hugely popular, and international MBA-toting managers and entrepreneurs are driving the reform of the country's economy at a previously unimaginable pace. Impersonal, objective-oriented approaches to management are becoming more commonly adopted. Yet, at the same time, the old ways are not disappearing. Rather, interesting fusions of Western and Chinese management styles are emerging.

We have been both encouraging and fostering the development of this trend. We believe that an objective approach to problem-solving is important. But we also believe there are other ways of looking at problems that produce more sustainable solutions. That means putting people back on center stage, and looking not just at their behavior or actions, but also at their attitudes. It involves, dare we say it, getting *personal*.

In truth, there is no way to take people out of a problem, because it is people who have to solve their own problems in the end. Consultants can advise, but the person who needs to fix the problem is the one who is caught up in it. As the Tang Dynasty philosopher Liu Yuxi (772–842) wrote in *A Discourse on Heaven*: "A capable man is he who can solve all problems." And by this he meant problems within himself as well as without.

We believe that the starting point for a corporate coach should be what we call the "human touch." This means looking at people, not at external factors, and helping them to develop their internal well-being. At the core of every problem, the capable coach looks for and finds people. We are not saying that external factors don't exist or should be ignored; we are simply saying that the needs of the person have to come first.

But perhaps we are getting ahead of ourselves here. Some readers might still be asking exactly what coaching is.

 ## THE INNER GAME

### DIFFERENT COACHES, DIFFERENT SOLUTIONS

Wang hadn't had a good education, but through dint of hard work he had climbed the ranks of a trading company from office assistant to deputy general manager. A capable man with a winning personality and good people skills, he earned recognition from his clients, colleagues, and even the board of directors.

When the general manager resigned, the board of directors appointed Wang. He was exhilarated – this was the goal he had been working toward for years. But at the same time he harbored feelings of insecurity. Other deputy managers, he thought, and some of his colleagues, held doctorates and master's degrees. Wang worried about how they would react to his promotion, and whether they would support him.

Wang discovered that different coaches responded to his dilemma in different ways. But they all listened to him, and used a questioning technique that aimed to uncover the truth, establish what his goals were, and help him to see for himself the problems that were holding him back.

*Coach A*: So, you never took a university degree?

*Wang*: No.

*Coach A*: But you still managed to work your way up from office assistant to deputy general manager, right? Did you need a degree to do that?

*Coach B*: Who appointed you general manager?

*Wang*: The board of directors.

*Coach B*: Why did they pick you?

*Wang*: Because they trust me.

*Coach B*: Well, if the board trusts you, why don't you trust yourself? Do you think the directors would appoint someone incompetent to take charge of their business?

*Coach C*: What does it mean for you to become general manager?

*Wang*: It's the goal I've been working toward; it's my dream.

*Coach C*: What's more important: your goal, or what others think?

*Wang*: Well, my goal.

*Coach C*: So?

*Wang*: I'll continue to work at reaching my goal, but I'm still worried.

*Coach C*: So, where's the problem? You can continue to worry as you work toward your goal!

*Coach D*: What are you worried about?

*Wang*: I don't have high educational qualifications, and I'm worried about what some of the others will say about that.

*Coach D*: Has it occurred to you that you are worrying more about your educational qualifications than about whether you are qualified for the job?

*Wang*: I suppose I'm worried about whether I'm qualified for the job.

*Coach D*: Is this worrying going to provide you with a degree? Will it change other people's opinions? Will it make you any more qualified for the job?

*Wang*: No...

*Coach D*: What's your goal?

*Wang*: To be general manager.

*Coach D*: Well, if that's what you want, is there anything else you might do besides worrying?

*Wang*: I could sign up for a degree course, and talk the issue through with my colleagues.

*Coach E*: Are you second-guessing your colleagues, or did they tell you that they don't think you're qualified for the job?

*Wang*: It's my own view, but I think they might be thinking along those lines.

*Coach E*: They might, or they might not. Right?

*Wang*: Yes, that's true.

*Coach E*: So, what can you do about it?

*Wang*: I could try to find out what they truly think.

Most of us, when we hear the word "coaching," think of sport. Coaches are those people who stand on the sidelines shouting encouragement to the athletes they have spent months, perhaps years, training in the lead-up to their public performances. Coaches, in other words, help athletes to realize their potential. They do this by guiding them through conversations and training techniques. A sports coach aims to help his athletes grow, and a good coach realizes that athletes only grow if they are learning for themselves.

In fact, it was a sports coach who was in part responsible for the emergence of corporate coaching. In the 1970s, Timothy Gallwey, a Harvard University English literature graduate, tennis player, and former U.S. Navy officer, published a tennis coaching book called *The Inner Game of Tennis*. Gallwey's revolutionary idea was that tennis coaching had traditionally concentrated on external factors such as technique. In reality, as Gallwey put it, "every game is composed of two parts, an outer game and an inner game." By concentrating on the person at the heart of the game, he argued, it was possible to help players win the inner game against themselves and instinctively learn confidence.

For many people at the time, Gallwey's theories seemed like so much mumbo-jumbo. A popular TV presenter in the United States, Harry Reasoner, decided to put them to the test. He invited Gallwey to appear on his show and teach tennis to an overweight woman named Molly.

Gallwey began by instructing Molly, who had never played tennis, to watch how balls he threw in her direction moved through the air. Next, he asked her to say aloud the word "bounce" every time the ball hit the ground. A few moments later, Gallwey told Molly to say the word "hit" every time she moved to return the ball. Within 15 minutes, Molly was moving around the court returning forehands and backhands as if she had been having tennis instruction for six months.

In other words, Molly had taught herself tennis by relying on her instincts, and figuring out what worked and what did not.

Days later, AT&T marketing director Archie McGill turned up in Los Angeles and, impressed with what he had seen on TV, invited Gallwey to put some of his marketing team through an "inner game" coaching session. Corporate coaching had been born.

Gallwey, who continues to work with a high-profile list of corporate clients, calls coaching "unlocking potential to maximize performance." And it wasn't long before the business world realized that his approach could be applied to the training of corporate leaders. Rather than trying to "show" people how to grow their business, coaches could help people to clarify their goals, uncover the truth about what is holding them back, shift their interfering mindsets, and then work with them to establish goals through listening, asking questions, making distinctions, and giving feedback. Rather than telling people what to do, coaches posed questions that helped the clients to find the answers for themselves, and to come up with their own solutions to difficulties they previously might not even have been aware they were facing.

As our coaches in China have found, it is a method that can work as well with children as with high-flying corporate managers.

The son of one of our coaches who goes by the name of Elsie was feeling overwhelmed by school and life, and by all the challenges they bring. Elsie thought for a while and then said to her son: "But you're not afraid when you play your video games, are you?"

"No," he said.

"Isn't it more exciting the bigger the monsters in the game are?"

Her son nodded.

"Well, maybe you need to think about the challenges you're facing as if they are monsters in one of your video games. All you've got to do is hit them hard and eventually they'll go away. Look at them, and say: 'Right, now it's time to have some fun.'"

"But what if I hit the monster and he hits me back harder? What if I fail?" he asked, clearly not convinced.

"Well, what do you do when you can't kill the monsters in your video games?" Elsie responded.

Her son looked confused and then smiled in sudden comprehension. "I start again," he said.

Elsie, in short, was concentrating on her son's inner game rather than his outer one. Instead of taking an "issues, not people" approach to the various problems that were troubling her son, she reached out to the person and asked questions that drew him back to how he as a person dealt with them.

## A CHINESE ENVIRONMENT

When Timothy Gallwey wrote *The Inner Game of Tennis*, one of the things reviewers were quick to comment on was its Zen-like quality. In fact, it is sometimes referred to today as the "Zen of tennis." This would probably be somewhat confusing for anyone who actually practices Zen – the Japanese name for a branch of Buddhism found also in China, Korea, and Vietnam. In the Chinese world Zen is known as *Chan*, and it emphasizes meditation as the path to enlightenment. In the West, by contrast, it has come to be seen as a way of unlocking spontaneity, mostly due to books such as the classic *Zen in the Art of Archery* by Eugen Herrigel.

But even if the idea of coupling Zen and tennis were to strike the average Chinese person as somewhat odd, the idea of harmonizing our inner and outer games would not. The turmoil of the 20th century has produced a China that is, of course, very different from the old dynastic China. But history and Chinese philosophical traditions continue to have a huge influence on the thinking and behavior of modern Chinese. To this day, no matter whether they are high-ranking Communist Party officials or go-get-it entrepreneurs, Chinese people pepper their conversations with phrases from the texts that have long been the backbone of a classical education. This bedrock of Chinese thought is shaped mostly by Confucianism, but also by Buddhism and Taoism. And while these three philosophical traditions are in many ways vastly different, they all share a preoccupation with harmonizing the inner and the outer self.

Confucianism is often misunderstood in the West as a religion, but it is better to understand it as a body of writings that provide guidance in relationships – no matter whether it is a father and his son, or heads of state and their subjects. In fact, some have charged that Confucianism's emphasis on people and relationships can lead to weaknesses in the rule of law in Confucian societies. Whether this is the case or not, Confucius was not a man who would have seen the sense in an "issues, not people" approach to problem-solving. Confucius asked people to look into themselves before they looked elsewhere for excuses: "When you have faults," he advised his followers, "do not fear to abandon them."

Confucius lived some five centuries before the birth of Christ in a time that is known poetically as the Spring and Autumn Period

(722–481 BC). (It actually takes its name from a literary classic, *The Spring and Autumn Annals*, which may have been written by Confucius.) It was a politically turbulent era before the unification of China as an empire, and Confucius spent most of his later years wandering from one kingdom to the next attempting to bend the ears of rulers who, for the most part, showed very little willingness to listen. His message was a code of behavior that he saw as providing the way to a unified China that could bestow prosperity on the people. At the risk of oversimplification, Confucius urged his followers to transform themselves through study, observation, and deep thought so that they could lead by example.

Although his attempts to influence the politics of his time were limited, in his twilight years Confucius assembled an increasing number of followers in his home-town of Qufu, in the northern Chinese province of Shandong. They are thought to have transcribed his sayings in a canon of classics – most famously, the *Analects* – that have made him the most influential thinker in the history of the Far East.

Meanwhile, two centuries after the death of Confucius, at about the same time his ideas were being adopted as the state religion, a new faith was beginning to percolate into China along the Silk Road.

Siddhartha Guatama is thought to have been born a minor prince in what is now modern Nepal in 563 BC, just 12 years after the birth of Confucius. His life as a small boy and into early adulthood was one of cosseted luxury, and he was married to a cousin at the age of 16. When he was 29, however, he saw four things that changed his life: a crippled old man, a diseased man, a decaying corpse, and a wandering ascetic. Suddenly perceiving that life was an unending cycle of birth, disease, and decay, Siddhartha renounced his life of luxury, his wife and child, and set off on a journey to discover how to overcome suffering. For six years, like many wandering ascetics in northern India of the time — and to this day — Siddhartha punished his body with harsh regimes of fasting and long bouts of isolated meditation. At the age of 35, however, he discovered a Middle Way – a path of moderation – and achieved an awakening while meditating under what is now called the Bodhi Tree. The historical Buddha's awakening was an insight into the nature of suffering and the discovery of a path that could lead to liberation from it. Initially, he was dubious that it could be taught, but after deciding to try and impart his message to humanity he gave a sermon at the Deer Park near modern-day Varanasi in northern India and the Buddhist monkhood was born.

When Buddhism started to filter into China from Central Asia some two centuries later, it must have seemed a very alien religion to the Chinese of that time. The Han Dynasty (206 BC – AD

220) had unified the nation and adopted Confucianism as the state philosophy, with an administration of scholars who underwent rigorous state examinations on the Confucian classics. The ideal Confucian scholar-administrator of the time was the Confucian gentleman, or *junzi* (literally, "son of a prince") who led by virtuous example, and who pursued personal perfection with the aim of producing a better society. The newly arrived Buddhists, on the other hand, seemed to advocate renunciation of the material world, and even called on young men to abandon their families and society for the meditative calm of the monastery.

All the same, as the centuries rolled by, the immigrant faith found more and more Chinese believers. By the time of the Tang Dynasty (618–907) – the apogee of ancient Chinese civilization – Buddhism was flourishing in China, and was adopted by the country's imperial leaders, until a clampdown on the all-powerful monasteries around the country in the eighth century sent the religion into a slow and finally terminal decline. If the Chinese revolution of 1949 had not signaled an end to public religious life, however, it is likely that – as in Hong Kong and Taiwan – China's Buddhist temples and monasteries would be busier places of worship than they are today, even though they are slowly coming back to life again.

After all, even if their aims differed, Confucianism and Buddhism shared a deep interest in personal development. For a Confucian scholar of ancient China, Buddhism might well have appeared as a set of precepts that added a spiritual dimension to the rules of self-development he lived by. But, as it turned out, Buddhism had another natural ally in traditional Chinese culture that eased its path to wide acceptance.

Taoism is the least understood of China's intellectual traditions – even by the Chinese themselves. It probably grew from a very ancient form of nature worship, but it became an influential philosophy through the writings of Laozi, a possibly mythical figure who is claimed by his followers to have been a contemporary of Confucius. For Laozi, *Dao*, or "the Way," is an ineffable force that orders the universe, and coexisting with it might best be translated into modern terms as something like "going with the flow." Laozi advocated the value of "action through inaction." By this he didn't mean doing nothing at all but, rather, spontaneously following the path that yields the best results – in other words, harmonizing our inner and outer games.

The language of philosophical Taoism is dense, subtle, and poetic, defying simple explanations. In fact, Laozi famously wrote that "the *Tao* that can be named is not the eternal *Tao*." But as a folk religion, Taoism spread to every corner of China and has been influential in countless traditional Chinese customs – acupuncture, traditional medicine, various kinds of fortune telling, kung fu and *qigong*, just to name a few. And although in doing so it had strayed some way from the original teachings of an Indian prince-turned-ascetic, Buddhism in China often piggybacked on the popularity of folk Taoism, with its worship of the venerable sage, Laozi, and a host of other supernatural beings. After all, like Buddhism, at its heart Taoism was a spiritual path that emphasized a personal relationship with the outside world.

There are no doubt those who would argue that these ancient Chinese beliefs have only a peripheral bearing on modern Chinese life. But, as we have said before, they are something of a bedrock in the Chinese mind. What's more, when we took coaching to China, it occurred to us that one thing China's philosophical traditions had in common was that the centricity of the person was all-important. Confucianism, Buddhism, and Taoism can all be used in developing one's potential. Their focus is the betterment of things through the betterment of the person.

Although Buddhism began in India, the way it is practiced in China can be traced back to the origins of Chinese civilization. Similarly, Taoism and Confucianism are products of Chinese culture as much as they have helped to shape it. And at the very root of this culture, it could be said, lies a single Chinese character: ren (人)

Understanding the origin and development of the character ren is therefore important in understanding the evolution of

Chinese thought, which in turn is important in understanding how modern coaching techniques can be fused with Confucianism, Taoism and Buddhism, to produce a new, successful people-oriented approach to problem-solving and personal development. This new management technique is already helping people in the newly emerging superpower of China become more successful. We know. We have seen it work. We call it the *Ren* Coaching Model.

##  IT'S ALL ABOUT *REN*

In 1899, a young Chinese professor in Beijing – or Peking, as it was then known in English – went to a traditional Chinese apothecary for some medicine. He was given a "dragon bone" – a common prescription – and told to grind it and digest it. "Dragon bones" were usually fossilized animal, or sometimes even dinosaur, bones, and on this bone the professor noticed some curious markings that looked like a form of writing distantly related to modern Chinese. It was an observation that led to the discovery of the seat of the ancient Shang Dynasty (1600–1064 BC) near a city called Anyang in northern Henan province – the Yellow River cradle of Chinese civilization.

The many more bones found near Anyang were "oracle bones" – ox scapulae and tortoiseshells that had been heated until they cracked in an ancient divination ceremony. For the priests who administered these ceremonies, the cracks that emerged on the bones provided divine answers to questions posed by the mortal world. After the ceremonies concluded, it is now believed, the questions and the answers were inscribed on the bones. A chance discovery by an observant Beijing professor had, in other words, led Chinese scholarship an important step closer to the origins of the Chinese written language.

For newcomers to China – and even many who are not – the sight of street signs, books, magazines, and newspapers covered in what look to be tiny pictures can be intimidating. And with many thousands of these "pictures" in everyday use, they are right to be intimidated. Linguists call this unique and very complex writing system logographic, as opposed to, say, English, which is alphabetic. That is another way of saying that, like the hieroglyphs of ancient Egypt, essentially every Chinese word is represented by its own unique symbol. Although we oversimplify the modern Chinese writing system at the risk of failing to understand it all, it is safe to say that many Chinese characters started out life directly as pictures of the things they represented.

This, it can be argued, is an even deeper bedrock of the Chinese mind than the faiths and philosophies that accompanied the rise of historical China, reaching deep into antiquity. If faiths and philosophies such as Confucianism, Taoism and Buddhism, are the bedrock of the Chinese mind, then the Chinese writing system is its core. It is the written language, after all, that unites the many dialects of modern China, so that a native of Beijing who understands barely a word of Cantonese can still pick up a local daily newspaper at a Hong Kong newsstand and read it front to back over a morning pot of green tea. What is more, this sense of a kindred culture in the written word has been a unifying force in the Chinese world for far longer than anywhere else in the world.

And so the character *ren*, like so many other characters in modern use, first appeared around 3,500 years ago. It looked somewhat different from its modern version, but the two variations are both clearly a person standing sideways:

*Ren -* "oracle bone" script of *human*
甲骨文的「人」字

*Ren - modern* Chinese of *human*
今天的「人」字

It is possible that the *ren* character we see on oracle bones was in its time a symbol of identity and status. The kings of the Shang Dynasty considered themselves to be the "one man," or "I, above others," and used the character to denote their superiority. It is also likely that in the Shang, and in the Zhou Dynasty that followed it, the slave-owning elite used the character to denote exclusivity. But whatever it may have meant to the Chinese of many thousands of years ago, as Chinese civilization evolved, the *ren* character we now recognize in modern Chinese came to stand for both any given person and for the essence of humanity – in other words, it translates words that in English range from "person" and "people" through "man" and "humanity." What is more, the *ren* character became a component in all other characters related to things human, as noted by the famous Han Dynasty scholar Xu Shen, author of the first Chinese dictionary nearly 2,000 years ago.

This fascinating aspect of the Chinese writing system has been very useful for us in helping Chinese to start thinking about what it means to be a person, and in helping them to transform behavior that might be holding them back. After all, the characters that feature the *ren* component contain all the potential for human development. Chinese scholars realized this long ago. They might, for example, point to the word "compassion," which not only contains the character component *ren* but is pronounced almost identically, with only a slight variation in tone. This, they argued, was evidence that compassion was defining of humanity, even extending their argument to the position that someone who lacks compassion is not human.

But what may have been obvious to scholars of yore, is often not so obvious today. Compared to the "oracle bone" script of three-and-a-half millennia ago, the components of modern Chinese characters have become more stylized, and the original logic of their construction is not always so easy to discern. It is still there, though. Let us, for example, put two *ren* side by side: this can be

*Bi* (比) - "oracle bone" script of *compare*

*Cong* (从) - 3 kinds of "oracle bone" script of *conform* or *follow*

*Bei* (北) - "oracle bone" script of *north*

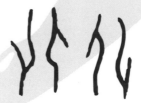

*Hua* (化) - 2 kinds of "oracle bone" script of *reform*

either *cong* (从), which means "conform" or "follow," or it can be *bi* (比), which means "compare." If, on the other hand, we put two *ren* back to back they become *bei* (北), which means "north" but in ancient times also meant "to turn against each other." And if we put two *ren* together with one facing forward and the other facing backward, the result is *hua* (化), which means "reform."

Within just these four basic concepts is already a host of meanings that we have found allows us to awaken our students to the possibilities inherent in the language they use every day and to the possibilities within themselves. If the evolution of the human mind is about realizing potential, we can find it all there already just in these four characters. Think about it: probably the starting point of all human awareness comes when we are able to compare two things – 比. From comparisons, we have polarities: good and bad, joy and sorrow, rich and poor, have and have not. This awareness evokes yearning, and sets off chain reactions of behavior.

Society, however, demands that our behavior adhere to established norms. In other words, we are being directed to 从 – to obey or conform. Of course, this is by no means an altogether bad thing. Often in our lives we find that we make enormous progress, or even breakthroughs, by modeling ourselves on or emulating people we admire and respect, or simply people who have mastery of a discipline or subject we have set our goals on. But conformity has its limits, and sooner or later we find ourselves starting to be limited by it. This generally is a source of disappointment. The person who once seemed to hold all the answers, we now realize only held some of them, and we find ourselves turning away from (北) – perhaps even against – them.

But perhaps one day we realize that this continual process of conformity, followed by a reaction away from it, is a never-ending cycle of conflict, and we begin to consider the notion that our behavior has to change of its own accord. We have, in other words, come to the concept of 化, or "reform." We are no longer following blindly before reacting in the opposite direction. Rather, we are listening to something inside ourselves – following our hearts, even. Confucianism, Taoism, and even Buddhism are, in other words, asking us to pay attention to our "inner game."

But before we return to that interesting analogy, let us take another look at the character for reform – 化 – because it is truly fascinating. It symbolizes a person standing upright and another twirling around, or changing their position and perspective. How often do so many of us forget that this is the essence of reform? Put another way, when people interact with the world, they have two choices – either to change the environment, or to change themselves. Recalling Confucius and the Taoist sage Laozi, when the former proves too difficult, all that is required is to take a "twirl" and respond to the changing environment.

There may be some, of course, who read this and say we are just playing games with words. In a sense, we are. But it is also a reminder that sometimes when we look afresh at the things around us that we take for granted, it can also help us to remember our own potential for change. In China we have found that having our students look again at the word *ren*, and at the many words in which it features, can help them to see anew their own potential. What is more, it brings us back to the human touch, with which we introduced this chapter. *Ren* reminds us that, whether our desire is to become better managers, colleagues, partners, or lovers, it all has to begin with the person at the center of the situation. 人

# PART 2

## *Ren*
## AT WORK

Chapter **2**

# Changing
# ATTITUDES

**S**trange things can happen when people enroll in a *Ren* Coaching program. Take Feng Jun, the 36-year-old CEO and founder of the consumer electronics and online music retailer Aigo. After seven years as a non-smoker, Feng, who was completing the *Ren* Coaching program in 2004, resumed the habit. He admits it was an unusual decision.

"People in coaching go through life-changing experiences," says Feng, a jovial and rotund man, given to peals of laughter. "Most of them who smoke decide to give it up. Maybe I'm not a good example of what can happen, but I have to tell the truth. That's one of the things you learn – not to lie to yourself, not to deceive yourself. And the fact is, I'd given up cigarettes for seven years, put on a lot of weight, and I missed smoking. To be honest, I'd been wanting to start again for seven years, but when I originally quit everybody around me was calling me a hero, and it became a kind of face issue. But I wasn't enjoying it, and later, I decided that as long as I didn't inconvenience anyone else with my smoking, why shouldn't I? So, I don't smoke at work, or when I'm eating out with other people who don't smoke, but if I'm at home or at a bar with friends who smoke, I light up."

Feng, who founded Aigo's Beijing-based parent company, Huaqi, with just 230 yuan (US$29) in 1993, now oversees a fast-growing business with annual sales of more than US$250 million. Products include mobile data storage, MP3 players, digital music downloads, and digital cameras. Feng's ambition for Aigo – the name is a stylized transliteration of *aiguo*, or "patriot" – is for the brand to become China's answer to Japan's Sony and Korea's Samsung, both of whom Aigo is outselling on the domestic market with its MP3 players. And as with an increasing number of influential Chinese business leaders, the *Ren* Coaching Model has changed the way Feng looks at himself and at the people he works with.

## OPENING UP AND SIGNING ON

Feng first heard about the *Ren* Coaching Model in 2004, when a former colleague began pestering him to sign up. At first he begged off, saying he was too busy. "I was working 18-hour days, and I couldn't see how this course could be worth me taking four days out of my busy schedule." But after hearing more testimonials from people whose attitude seemed to have taken a drastic turn for the better while undergoing coaching, Feng became intrigued and enrolled.

"I couldn't believe, in that first course, how open everybody became, how people stood up in front of a crowd of complete strangers and began to reveal things about themselves, to tell everybody openly what had gone wrong in their lives. We had people getting up and telling everybody about problems they had with their family members, their mothers, their fathers, their friends and colleagues. This is not something you usually see happen. You suddenly begin to realize that everybody has troubles, their own unique story. Problems with friends, problems with family, problems everywhere. Usually, these are things we keep secret, but when everybody is standing up and talking about it, you start to think, why not? Why shouldn't I? It's a situation in which you discover that everybody is different, and everybody is similar.

And I began to get a better understanding of human psychology. This is something you gain. You realize that, at heart, everybody is the same, and at the same time they're completely different."

Like so many other Chinese who have experienced the *Ren* Coaching program in recent years, Feng signed up for the whole program on the spot. "I could see from the start," says Feng, "that it's a value chain. If you only do one part of it, you can't really understand what it's about. But if you see it through, you learn many things not only about yourself, but about what coaching itself is about. If you only do the first part of the program, all you know is that something happened, but you don't know *what* happened or *why*. See it through, and it becomes clear what happened and why."

Chen Baofang, president of the Yuewang Jewelry Group, a growing chain of more than 40 custom-made jewelry stores based in Zhejiang province, sees it the same way. "I could see that to get results, to see the true intention of the courses, you were going to have to make your way all the way through. You wouldn't be able to see the value otherwise. Of course, there were going to be moments of doubt, but it was only by completing the whole thing that you were going to get the answers to those doubts."

# ATTITUDE SHIFTS

What happens, everyone who has completed the program agrees, is that attitudes get changed. As Jason Yan, vice-president of Beijing-based Focus Media, puts it: "I can't say I've learned much in the way of management skills from the *Ren* Coaching Model, because that's not really what coaching is about. Coaching is about the way you deal with people and things, about attitude, not about skills. If you ask what skills I picked up while in coaching, I would have to say that I didn't really pick up any, but it *did* change my attitude. I've become more positive, I see more possibilities, and I look for more ways to solve problems."

Yan has played a pivotal role in China's fastest-growing media operation. In the space of less than three years, according to Yan, Focus Media has grown from a business valued at 50 million yuan (US$6.2 million) to a media group valued at US$2.5 billion, by tapping a previously neglected media advertising channel – public TVs (largely in elevators) and LED billboards in shopping districts. With more than 10,000 clients, Focus Media's turnover has grown from around 60 million yuan (US$7.5 million) in 2003 to a projected 1.6 billion yuan (US$199 billion) in 2006, making it China's third-biggest media group after state-owned China Central Television (CCTV) and Shanghai Media Group (SMG). But despite the phenomenal success of Focus, Yan says coaching has personal applications that have made it worthwhile for him.

"It's something that helps you to overcome your inflexibilities, see yourself better, and understand just where your business is at. It also confronts you with your psychological weaknesses, and that can be extremely uncomfortable. At one point, I nearly walked out, but the people I was on the course with talked me out of it because it's like a highly solidified community, in which everybody counts, and that in itself is an important thing to experience. We all have people we like and people we don't like, but in coaching you learn that to be successful you have to be tolerant of lots of kinds of people. We're mixing with some of the most outstanding people in China, but outstanding people aren't necessarily all like us. Everybody has different thinking and different styles, but we have to adopt the same goals in order to move ahead together. So, tolerance is really important."

Yuewang Jewelry's Chen Baofang had a similar experience early in his coaching experience. Despite much resistance to what he was seeing around him, he says, he also had revelations about himself and his behavior.

"I realized," he says, "that many of us, including myself, tend to be conceited about ourselves, and much of that is based on how we see our own experience. Our past experience tells us we're okay because in the past I did this or that, and we flaunt that experience. But with other people this tends to become a way of looking down on them. Because you did this in the past, I don't trust you, or I don't want to be your friend. But if you're forever stuck in the past, in terms of other people, you tend to be stuck with negative things. It's easy, after all, to see other people's weaknesses, even their assets, but this determines how you interact with them. So one of the things you get out of coaching is that you start to look at people with tolerance, with appreciation. If you cultivate this habit, it changes everything: how you interact with your entire network of people, including your colleagues."

"Experience generally makes us inflexible," says Focus Media's Jason Yan. "It teaches us to be constantly making distinctions about what is right and what is wrong, and that makes it difficult for us to listen to our employees. While they're talking, we've already passed judgment and don't hear them out. The big difference in me now is that I can listen to people without bringing my personal judgment into the equation; I can have some open communication before making judgments."

 ## CENTRALIZATION VERSUS COMMUNICATION

For Yan, this is a change that is helping to break down what he sees as the traditional centralization of Chinese companies.

When dialog becomes part of the management process, he says, responsibility starts to devolve away from a single overarching leader, which is the pattern in so many private-sector Chinese enterprises.

"Often, you have one person making all the decisions and setting the direction of the business," says Yan. "Companies can grow very quickly that way, but once that person starts making mistakes they can go down just as quickly. This tends to limit the life spans of businesses in China. But this centralized model is changing, and local businesses are starting to evolve. And mostly it's because people are starting to listen and hear alternative opinions."

Yuewang's Chen points out that when leaders rule from above and don't listen to employees, they lose touch with the realities of the business they are trying to run. "Coaching teaches you that you can bridge the gap with people quickly," he says. "It is possible to sit down with two employees and within five minutes make changes, have them trust you, and be willing to speak openly about how they feel. The alternative, perhaps, is your employees fear you, and tell you nothing about what they are thinking. But if you win their trust, you can pretty much get to the bottom of anything – what they think of, say the management structure, and what they think can be changed."

"A lot of Chinese companies are family businesses," says Yan. "They grow to a certain point and then meet obstacles. The *Ren* Coaching Model concentrates heavily on this problem, and can help businesses like that grow by changing attitudes. For people who've not had much experience in society, these courses don't have much impact; but for someone who's got rich experience, who thinks they know what they're doing, coaching can have a hugely moving impact."

## ATTITUDES AND POSSIBILITIES

Yan calls coaching "a communicative culture" that is all about "finding possibilities." Becoming part of that, he says, is all about people changing their attitudes.

"I was down in Ningbo recently, visiting the sales director of the Peacebird Group," Yan says. "He started telling me about a course he had attended in Shanghai. I asked him what kind of course, and he said it had to do with attitude. 'Oh,' I said. '*Ren*.' Amazed, he asked me how I knew, and once we got talking about my own experience, the distance between us disappeared altogether because we suddenly had a common language."

Yan points out that a common language is key to cooperation. "In China, cooperation has always been a particular problem. But more and more people are talking now about 'win-win', 'win-win-win,' and all kinds of multiple-win scenarios. There's a logic to this.

If somebody keeps losing at a game, they won't play with you anymore. So, there's strength in cooperation. If you have an understanding with your partner, can communicate with them, you can reach consensus and reach goals. Maybe it's hard for us to completely change, but we can change our weaknesses if we're aware of them, and making us aware of our weaknesses and learning to adjust them is precisely what coaching does."

Like Yan, Aigo president and founder Feng Jun is quick to point out that the *Ren* Coaching Model is not about helping people to acquire skills but about helping them to change their attitudes.

"China's private sector has never lacked skills. We understand China; we understand the policies of the government, and how to deal with them. The problem is that people's attitudes are fixed. It's like the difference between being positive and being negative is so small, and yet the two things are a thousand kilometers apart," he says.

# Chapter 3

# Finding
# OPPORTUNITIES
# in CRISIS

W hen Vantage Gas Appliance Stock Co. CEO Huang Qijun told 24 of his executives in April of 2003 that he wanted them to participate in a corporate coaching course, they were surprised. Vantage, after all, had been China's leading producer of gas stoves for some eight years, and with business going so well, what was the point of embarking on a program of "training"? Most of the executives concluded that the exercise would likely be a waste of time.

From the start, it was clear that Vantage was no ordinary challenge for a team of coaches – and not simply because the management saw no room for improvement. Just a few months earlier, Zhongshan, where Vantage was headquartered, was one of three cities in Guangdong province that had reported clusters of what at the time was called "atypical pneumonia." On January 2, a local chef checked into Zhongshan No. 2 Hospital short of breath and feeling feverish. Although he was put in isolation, he still infected 13 hospital staff, who in turn infected 15 other Zhongshan residents. By the time the disease had acquired a name – Severe Acute Respiratory Syndrome (SARS) – from a World Health Organization Italian doctor, who himself succumbed to the disease, hundreds of people in Guangdong were sick. As the disease fanned out across China, and via international flights out of Hong Kong to the rest of the world, the mood in Guangdong was grim. With everyone shunning public places, the *Ren* Coaching team frequently found themselves taking lunch in deserted restaurants. At the gates to Vantage's headquarters, guards took the temperatures of everyone who came and went.

SARS cast a shadow over everyone's lives in those days, and people were afraid to mix with each other. Public events were canceled, and workers hurried home after work, shuttering themselves away indoors to track the progress of the disease on TV. The city streets were deserted. Meanwhile, Vantage had set itself production targets that were 30%-50% higher than for the same period in the previous year.

##  "TEACHING PEOPLE TO FISH"

From a coaching perspective, the challenge at Vantage was to identify opportunities and possibilities that no one had yet seen. Everyone had a different outlook on SARS, after all. The boss of one local foreign-invested Zhongshan company reassured his workers that now that SARS was all over the media, the really dangerous period had come to an end – it was while the disease was still unknown that everyone was at most risk. Now that society was mobilized, he told them, the dangers were diminished. Meanwhile, the manager of a local electronics store told his staff that, to be sure, with SARS raging, very few people were willing to venture out to go shopping, but those that did come out to shop definitely wanted to buy something.

These viewpoints illustrate that the dangers and risks posed by any crisis are largely a matter of attitude. And the *Ren* Coaching team took the position that it was essential to adopt a winning attitude to SARS, or risk panic and a loss of direction.

But at Vantage, an equal challenge for the coaching team was the company's management. With a staff of more than 1,000 and an annual turnover of hundreds of millions of yuan, Vantage may only have been operating for 10 years but it was already a very established business. To become a market leader in such a short space of time was no small feat, but it also meant that the company culture had roots that ran deep and were already difficult to shift. As an ancient Chinese expression has it, "well water and river water do not run together," which is a way of saying that at Vantage every department was a law unto itself. Moreover, very few Vantage employees could see the point of bringing in a coaching team, given that the company had been No. 1 in its field for so long. The first job for the coaching team, in other words, was to get Vantage management on side. But from the start the coaching team was met with suspicion and confusion, as if to say, "We've been managing for so many years now; what can all this stuff possibly bring in the way of positive change?"

As leadership theorists point out, adaptive work requires cohesion between the entire workforce and leadership because it often involves shifting fixed values and thinking, while at the same time adopting an open attitude to learning. This isn't easy, because it is often difficult for us to discard even outmoded patterns of thought. Compounding the problem at Vantage was the fact that managers suddenly found themselves facing not one but two adaptive challenges: the threat of SARS and the challenge of adapting to a coaching environment.

It was clear to the coaching team from the outset that there was resistance to the very idea of coaches coming into the company. The initial workshops were unruly, with many staff either turning up late or not turning up at all. With attendance levels at a low ebb, the message coming back to the coaches was that the Vantage team was too busy with work to attend. Meanwhile, those that did attend were listless and unengaged, as if the workshops were a chore they had to endure – very few attendees exhibited a will to learn.

## TIME TO SHOUT "STOP!"

It was time, the coaching team decided, to shout "Stop!", rather as a sports coach might when the athlete he is training is doing everything wrong. The main reason for shouting "Stop!" is to carry out a review, and the point of a review is to improve efficiency. As far as the coaching team was concerned, they were dealing with a situation where the Vantage staff were not taking coaching seriously, had no clear idea of its value, and as a result had no idea of where the things they were being asked to learn were supposed to be taking them.

As we have noted already, coaching is about people, not issues. Coaching is about supporting people to grow, and improving their efficiency through that growth. Coaching's area of specialization has nothing to do with the kind of specialized knowledge that is required of people who work in, say, the gas appliances industry, but is specifically about people. Meanwhile, coaching-style leadership is typically non-experts leading the experts, or adaptive leadership (about attitudes and beliefs), as opposed to technical leadership (about methods and skills). As a Chinese expression has it, coaching is about teaching people to fish, rather than giving them fish.

Another important aspect of coaching is that it is not outer-directed. It doesn't look for external, environmental reasons for things being the way they are, but is inner-directed, seeking out inner potential in order to open up possibilities. In this sense, coaching is like the study we do before we start studying; it provides the client with the will to learn.

And the problem at Vantage was that virtually no one seemed to have the will to learn.

The *Ren* Coaching team knew it had to bring about a change in the attitudes of the Vantage management, or the whole coaching plan would simply fizzle out. At the same time, it was essential that guidance be given in workshops to help the management understand that a coaching workshop was something very different from a regular work meeting. In other words, it was not simply a question of shouting "Stop!", but also about working harder to change the attitudes that were standing in the way of engaging with learning and growth. Only when those attitudes changed could the situation start to change.

Vantage CEO Huang Qijun was a crucial player during this difficult time. Huang had a deep sense of the value of coaching, and had insisted that it be introduced into the workplace despite the resistance from management. It was a conviction that came of personal experience. In 2002, some 70 Vantage employees had participated in a training session that resulted in Vantage meeting a difficult target it had set for itself. Huang set about assembling a mobilization committee to establish collective goals, asking both individuals and the group to make a commitment. He also met with key players in the coaching course and worked to get them on-side.

Gradually the situation began to turn around. Even more importantly, as the coaching courses intensified, the participants began to get a better sense of what they were about and their outlook began to change.

## A CHANGE OF HEART

Some people, however, were tough nuts to crack. One of Vantage's most senior engineers objected strongly to the methods employed in the coaching courses. At the time, his team had been working unsuccessfully on an ultra-light water heater, and the coaches took this as an opportunity to see if they could make him see the value of coaching. They used a game that is designed to help people see the difference between technical, skills-base problems and attitude problems. The 24-strong engineering team was split up into four smaller teams, and each team was given four different-colored balls. The balls had to be passed from one person to the next in a specified order according to their colors. The result was chaos, with balls mis-passed and dropped, and one team taking as long as 38 seconds to complete the exercise. (The record is said to be 0.22 seconds.) A target was set for the Vantage teams to complete the exercise in one second, using whatever methods they could come up with, and eventually the target was reached by every team. For some of the participants, it was a moment of insight: they suddenly realized the impact a shift in attitude and outlook could have on an outcome. And when the senior engineer saw his co-workers coming up with inventive ways to solve problems, he found himself coming around to coaching's ability to achieve positive change.

The engineer wasn't the only one to have a change of heart. Other Vantage managerial staff started to become interested. Many began to discover that coaching-style listening was a powerful tool for achieving insight into problems. They began to discriminate between regular work meetings and coaching workshops, and increasingly they began to integrate coaching techniques into their regular daily management duties. As their attitudes changed, they also began to find novel ways to solve problems.

"In the beginning, I thought this was just another training method," said one Vantage division manager. "I never imagined it could have such a profound impact on our lives."

"It wasn't until I saw the changes in some of my colleagues that I realized coaching could be a useful tool and began to accept it," said another. "When one person starts to change, they bring others along with them, which produces even more change. It's like a ripple effect."

Shouting "Stop!" had achieved its goal. It helped the coaching team through a difficult juncture, winning over the clients and enabling a coaching culture to begin to take root in the business.

A Buddhist saying goes, "When the students are ready, a teacher will appear." So it was at Vantage. It wasn't until the management were ready to learn that the learning could begin.

 ## THINKING ANEW

To achieve unexpected results, it is necessary to adopt different methods and to seek out different methods, it is necessary to come up with new ways of thinking. When we get stuck in tried-and-tested, yet unproductive patterns of behavior, we are in a no-win situation. Innovation is the only way to move beyond a no-win situation, and all innovation is about innovative thinking; this is the value of a shift of thinking.

When Vantage found itself confronted not only by SARS, but also by the challenge of meeting its target of achieving a massive boost in sales, innovation was clearly the only way forward.

SARS was a terrible conundrum for everyone in business. In order to minimize the risks of being infected, shoppers were basically staying home. For businesspeople in China it was a nightmarish situation. As one Vantage manager put it in a coaching workshop, "If the shops are empty, tell us who we're going to sell our products to?"

When such a question is asked in a coaching environment, it is a hypothetical statement of a belief: If the shops are empty, it is impossible to do business. For a coach, however, this provides an opportunity to ask questions that can help the client break through a closed train of thought. The coach asks: "If the shops are empty, does that necessarily mean that there is no one who needs to buy things?" The answer to this question, of course, is: "No." The coach then asks. "If consumers still have needs but are afraid to go out shopping because of SARS, then what can we do?" For an experienced sales manager, the answer to this question is obvious: "We take the product to the customer."

In such ways are new possibilities recognized. Before too long, Vantage had set up a door-to-door delivery service for its products. It was also a service that would last beyond the duration of SARS.

The *Ren* Coaching team was coaching a change of attitude. It was asking the clients, "If the environment is this way, then what can be done to adapt to the environment?" At the same time, the team was using inspirational techniques to help Vantage staff find new ways of thinking and of doing things. It was well known, for example, that a bra factory in Guangdong province had nimbly switched from manufacturing bras to producing gauze face masks, which were now in such huge demand that the company's supply was unable to meet demand. Trucks were backed up in long queues outside the former bra factory's gates waiting for the masks to come off the production lines.

The coaching team discussed this example with Vantage management, and they began to think about other ways profits could be maximized in the midst of a crisis. While it was clear that switching from the production of gas stoves and heaters to face masks wasn't a realistic option, Vantage did have a product – originally one of the company's poorest sellers – that might have a chance in a SARS-spooked market. The product was a sterilization cabinet, and Vantage began to promote the stocks it had warehoused, while simultaneously developing a new model in rapid time. The market's response was overwhelming, and in no time at all the product had sold out.

As the benefits of innovation became increasingly obvious, Vantage began stepping up its campaign to take advantage of the SARS crisis. One thing the management discovered was that hand-washing liquid was in short supply, so a team was put in charge of sourcing hand-washing liquid to provide as giveaways with other Vantage products.

The result was that Vantage's May sales increased more than 50% on the previous year. But the best results came in June. Two days before the close of the month's sales, Vantage had sold 3 million more units than it had targeted, an increase of over 46% on the previous year. Meanwhile, on June 27, Vantage sold 6.7 million units, its record for a single day.

It was proof of a coaching maxim, "Coaching creates an environment through dialog." But it also recalled something Mao Zedong had said: "Dangerous crags provide endless vistas, and perhaps without that danger there would be no vistas either."

## LEARN, LEARN, LEARN

As a leading market player, Vantage would sometimes invite management consultants to help it with strategy and sales. But because the company wasn't cohesive, there was internal interference that made it difficult to effect change. The senior management in every department had their own ways of thinking and their own points of view, and this created all kinds of problems when implementing strategy.

At the core of corporate coaching is the equation "performance equals potential minus interference $(P = p - i)$." In other words, any organization has the potential for outstanding performance $(P)$, and this can be achieved by stimulating potential $(p)$ through reducing interference $(i)$. Coaching, then, is mostly about eliminating interference. If departments are not cooperating, and are complaining about each other, results are of course diminished. Coaching brings about changes of attitude that bring departments together through consensus, helping them collectively to meet targets.

An important coaching technique is providing clients with feedback. A feedback allows the client to discover things about themselves, rather than to become fixated on their environment. It is rather like a mirror that illuminates the client's blind spots, helping them make adjustments to their behavior. For example, one Vantage employee was renowned for his explosive temper, his constant arguments, and his inability to listen to others' opinions. The coach told him, "Actually, I sensed that you're very insecure. Do you have the confidence to listen to other people's opinions?"

A client may initially find such a critical feedback difficult to accept. But as time passes, despite their discomfort, they begin to find that direct feedback can help them to grow and to improve in their work. They begin to see that a coach's feedback can have long-term benefits, and they begin to accept them. In a very real sense, it is proof of another coaching maxim: "Everybody makes the best decision for themselves."

Three months of once-a-week coaching workshops at Vantage changed the way staff thought about their responsibilities. In the past, everyone knew that departmental goals were related to the overall goals of the company, but in their actions they concentrated only on their own departments. Coaching made the staff more sensitive to the business's overall goals and improved communication between departments.

One day, after the coursework had wound up, a *Ren* coach rang the Vantage accounting department to see how things were going. The department was in a meeting, so the coach rang another former client at Vantage. In passing, he mentioned that he had just called the accounting department, and the former client told him the latest sales figures. In the past, the former client admitted, he would never have been able to do this because Vantage's various departments were not in the habit of sharing information. There had been a lot of changes since the coaching courses had ended, he said. Everyone now had shared goals, and those shared goals meant sharing information.

"Sometimes," says Vantage's human resources manager Zhang Yuan, "a single idea can change everything in your life."

# Chapter 4

# From
# **CHAOS** to
# **PROSPERITY**

**W**hen Tang Liqin, a *Ren* coach, first returned to the Dalong Chemical Fertilizer Co. – a family business run by her father – in the remote northeastern province of Heilongjiang in 2002 for the first time in many years, she was shocked by what she saw. "My first impression was that it was a garbage dump, a ruined place," she says. "The company's warehouses were all overstocked with out-of-date fertilizer, and all the staff had glum, unhappy expressions, as if they were suffering from deep depression."

Apart from a few senior management staff, no one at the factory would even talk to the daughter of the "old man." She spent a week trying to figure out what was wrong with the place, and attempting to make contact with the workers, before acknowledging that her original plan to spend a month helping her father would achieve nothing. "I realized that, in such a short space of time, I would never figure out what had gone wrong, the problem was so severe." Tang went back to Shenzhen and quit her job with TopHuman. If she was going to help her father, she decided, she was going to have to do it full time.

Dalong's 166,000-square-meter factory grounds were ruined and neglected. The walls were crumbling, and the gate was falling apart and rusted. The workers worked in a derelict, crumbling structure, and even though a new one had been built and had a roof, it looked as if the workers had given up on the interior halfway through the job. The company was a far cry from its glory days. There was once a time in Heilongjiang when the very word "Dalong" – or "Great Dragon" – commanded respect. But those days were long gone.

 ## IN SEARCH OF HOPE

"It was terrifying at first," says Tang. "When I first came up for a look around, management staff would stroll over and chat with me from time to time. But when they discovered that I'd come up for good and my brief was to turn around the business, their attitudes changed completely. I got the feeling that they were panicked, as if they had something to hide, and were afraid they might get caught out."

This wasn't far from the truth. It didn't take Tang long to discover that the entire operation, from the lowliest floor sweepers to the section chiefs, who controlled the company's purse-strings, could be divided into three factions. One faction was responsible for production, another for business operations and sales, and the third for finances. Each faction, until Tang's arrival, essentially did whatever it pleased. If you belonged to a faction, you followed the leader of that faction, and you were not allowed to talk to anyone in any of the other factions. If you broke that rule, the next week you were out of a job. "The staff were all pressured into silence. The atmosphere was so unpleasant, it was almost impossible to bear."

It didn't take long for Tang's arrival to bring about at least one small change in this situation. Even though they didn't know her personally, the faction leaders had heard stories about Tang from her father, and they sensed she was going to be a formidable opponent and difficult to deal with. This motivated them to put their squabbles behind them and to unite in opposition. They shelved the tooth-and-nail fighting that had previously defined their working relationship, and not long after Tang arrived they confronted her, jabbing their fingers in her face and shouting, "Within three months we'll drive you back to Shenzhen!"

At first Tang was overwhelmed with a sense of hopelessness. She had no way of making contact with the ground-floor staff. Even those who lived in the same dormitory as she did were afraid to open their mouths in greeting, let alone make conversation. The only way they could make contact with Tang was to slip her a note or post her a letter. One young woman who lived opposite Tang wanted to make contact with her, but the only way she could do so was to make a trip to the city and post a letter from the post office. And Tang got not just one letter but a host of them from other staff members too. She began to sense that many of the staff cared about the company, and felt their desperation at being stuck in what looked to be such a hopeless situation. Tang wanted to respond to their letters. Unable to talk to anyone face to face, she enlisted several assistants who became the key actors in turning the situation around. Tang replied to the letters and then gave them to her assistants, who did all they could to make sure they reached their intended recipients. Tang joked that her assistants were her underground guerrilla force.

In the meantime, however, Tang's father wasn't quite ready to relinquish full control of the company. He had heard some of the grumblings about his daughter, and he was worried that opposition to her was mounting. Isolated from the management, he was concerned that she would be overwhelmed. But Tang was determined not to give up. She decided to use her coaching skills to try and make him see the need to make a choice.

"Why did you have me come up here?" Tang asked her father.

"Well, of course I wanted you to come up here," he replied. "With the company in a mess like this, the whole thing could fall apart tomorrow. If you didn't come up, what was going to become of the whole thing?"

"So, what's your objective?"

"That's simple enough. To get the company back on its feet."

"That's a good start. So what do you want me to do?"

"Do what you think is best."

From a coaching perspective, with just a few questions, Tang had made her father's true goal clear to him. Once his goal was clear, Tang told him what she had come up with in the course of her investigations, and then told him about the plan she intended to put into action. She even included her plans for dealing with the management.

Her father wasn't happy. "I don't think that's what you're here to do," he said. "I just wanted you to sort things out with the employees."

"The management problems in this company are being caused not just by the way the employees are being managed, but also by how the managers are managing themselves," Tang replied. "If you want me to sort things out with the employees, I've also got to deal with the relationships these managers have and make some adjustments."

Her father said he thought Tang was making something out of nothing, and told her he wasn't willing to support her if she took on the management of the company.

"You had me come up here because you trusted my ability," Tang responded. "But now that I'm telling you what I really think, you say you don't trust me, and you won't support me. If it's going to be like that, then I simply can't help. Either I go back to Shenzhen or I stay, but if I stay I've got to take some risks."

Her father hesitated, and Tang waited patiently while he weighed things up in his mind. Finally, he said: "Well, if you succeed it will be an unexpected dividend for me. If you fail, the company goes down, which is what looks like is going to happen anyway."

With this tacit approval to go ahead, Tang began to draw up her plans. Clearly the "gang of three" was the biggest problem. From their perspective, a stranger had turned up at the factory, and was threatening their positions and incomes. But Tang was curious as to why they saw her as such a dangerous threat, and so she started to dig. She found that all three of the managers came from the countryside, and from families that were far from well-to-do. But within a year of joining Dalong, each of them had a house and a car, and two of them had divorced their wives, one paying a settlement of 200,000 yuan (US$24,940). Tang checked the company accounts, and found that a lot of the expense claims the managers had been filing looked to be cooked up. They required only two signatures by management. Tang changed this system so that she was the only one with the power to authorize a payment. The managers responded with a smear campaign, spreading vicious rumors about Tang.

"It was really a messy situation, and there were times when I even thought of giving up," says Tang. "The company was so huge that it wasn't something I could sort out on my own. I had no support. Every night after work I'd go back to my dormitory and lay there hugging my quilt and crying. I had to force myself to face the situation, and try and rally my conviction that I was doing the right thing. Every morning, when I walked through the door, I'd do my best to face the employees with high spirits. How I appeared to the staff was simply too important to be any other way. In a sense, my existence there was the company's only hope, and if *I* couldn't face it, then I could hardly expect the employees to be able to."

With the odds stacked against her, Tang's strategy for dealing with the management triumvirate might have come from the pages of a classic Taoist text: she didn't strike back. She sensed that hitting directly back at them might do more harm than good to the business, so she adopted an attitude of calm goodwill and tolerance. When she got to the bottom of how the managers had been skimming company funds, she let them know what she knew, and also indicated that it would have to be made public if they stayed on, but she made no attempt to attack their reputations. All three managers resigned. It was rather like pushing hands in *tai chi*. In the end, it wasn't Tang, but those who were pushing against her, who took the brunt of their actions. The more force they exerted, the more that force came back at them.

 ## PUTTING A SYSTEM IN PLACE

With the management cabal broken, Tang was finally in a position to do the real work that needed to be done. The most pressing need was to rebuild the company's entire management structure, and establish an ISO9000 quality management system. In the space of a year Tang wrote tens of thousands of words, coming up with regulations and guidelines for a new structure.

This was new territory for her chairman father, who didn't like systems. His was a private-sector company, not a regulation-bound, state-run enterprise, he said. In his company, he thought his word should be final. If there were too many rules, he would no longer be free to put his ideas into practice. But once again, Tang used her coaching skills to bring him around.

"In your company do you want the freedom to be able to manage your staff, or do you want your staff to have the freedom not to be managed?"

A look of confusion flitted across his face.

"If there's no system, the staff are all completely free," said Tang, pushing her point home.

It was a point Tang's father had never considered, and he claimed he didn't see the logic of it. However Tang saw it, her father still would have nothing to do with the system she was trying to put in place.

"Well," said Tang. "You're free not to support me on this, and if the staff react badly to it you're also free not to intervene. But you have to support my methods, and stand with me on my position."

In the end, her father relented, and Tang went ahead with her plan. Extensive previous management experience made her qualified to make the necessary changes, but she says it is unlikely she could have put the plan into action without her coaching skills, which turned out to be crucial for dealing with the reactions from the staff. It is a huge change for everyone concerned when an organization puts a new management system in place. And when change is in the air, everyone responds differently – some people are optimistic, others pessimistic. And such was the case at Dalong.

In 2003, Tang set about promoting her ISO9000 quality management system by joining together with a consultancy. Her plan was that Dalong would put the system in place and then get national accreditation. But no one thought this was possible, as the company's original management system was such a mess. Basic management systems had only recently been put in place, and everyone was still getting used to them – never mind, they argued, putting an ISO9000 system in place. For ISO purposes, everything needed to be standardized, data-banked, and tabulated – it seemed to most people to be a mission beyond Dalong's reach.

Tang was adamant it could be done. "First of all," she says, "we *had* to do it. If we were going to be pessimistic about this, then we might as well just return to the ad-hoc way we did things in the past. My position was that there was no point in thinking about what was possible and what was not. It was far better just to put everything we had into giving it a shot. If there were going to be problems along the way, we'd figure out what to do about them when we got to them."

Five months on, an internal appraisal was carried out. To everyone's surprise, in many respects, progress was being made, even if from an outsider's perspective the company was still a long way from meeting ISO standards. Unfortunately, for many of the staff, it was the latter that seemed more significant, and they argued that this only proved they were right in the first place – it simply could not be done. Again, Tang brought her coaching experience to bear, and gave the staff a pep talk.

 ## COACHING GETS RESULTS

"If we pull this off – if we get accreditation – we've achieved our goal, and I believe we can definitely do this. But if we don't do it, then everything we've done in the past five months is wasted. In actual fact, we've already achieved concrete results. You choose. Do we go for it, or do we give up?"

That very month, in a massive concerted effort, Dalong employees put everything in place that had been missing when the internal appraisal was carried out, and the company got its ISO accreditation. When the news came through, a wave of excitement washed through the Dalong corridors, and everyone spontaneously broke into applause.

"It was a moment when I really felt the joy my colleagues were experiencing from achieving something they originally thought was impossible. During the three years I was at Dalong, from 2002 to 2005, there were times when secretly I also felt that the things everyone was saying were impossible really *were* impossible. But I also know that, if you make a leap of faith and take risks, impossible things can happen. As a coach, I'd always felt it was simple – success or failure was really just about conviction, and it was a choice. So, as a manager – even if the staff didn't know it – I was actually using coaching techniques. That I was able, within those three years, to produce the results I did for the company, to bring it back into the black, foster a team spirit, and create a vigorous, positive atmosphere, was all due to coaching. It was living proof that, when you're ready to believe in your ability to get things done, that ability becomes more powerful. At Dalong I did everything I could to radiate conviction and passion, and the staff saw that. One person's attitude and convictions can make a huge difference."

 ## THE PEOPLE FACTOR

One day Tang noticed that one of her employees looked to be going through her days like an automaton, moving from one task to the next with no passion or motivation. Tang approached her.

"Are you clear about why you come to work?" she asked the employee. "Have you ever thought about what you might do with this platform; where you might like to end up?"

"No," said the employee. "I just got the job. After I started, I felt I was improving and that I wanted to continue in this line of work. But then I started to feel unmotivated, as if I was numbed. I know my attitude is bad. I come to work when it's time to come to work, and when it's time to leave, I go home. I don't know where I want to be or what direction I really want to take."

"Don't you feel like you're lacking something in your life?" Tang asked.

"Lacking something?" said the employee, looking surprised.

"Have you ever thought about cars? Sometimes we're driving a car and the ignition cuts out. We have to call for a towing truck and get it fixed somewhere, or perhaps we have to get out and push and get it started that way. But eventually we get the car going again. All the same, whether we tow it to a garage or we get out and push, the car doesn't get itself going – *we* have to do it, and if we don't, that car is stopped for good. Actually, we people are exactly the same. We've all got an engine we have to get going sometimes. And when our goal is unclear, it's as if we're lacking an engine. The people around us, our colleagues and superiors, will all worry about us – they'll even get out and push us to try and get us moving. But if we're not out pushing ourselves, then we're a stalled car. So, if we're talking about how to perform better at work and get results, what's most important to you?"

"I want to find my engine," the employee laughed. "I don't want my boss to be pushing me along every day."

For Tang, this became the "engine story" and she shared it often with her colleagues at Dalong. So many engines had got stalled at the chemical fertilizer factory run by her father, and while many of those engines started again on their own as Tang set about her ambitious program of getting the company back up on its feet, some needed a little coaching assistance.

When Tang first arrived in Heilongjiang and things were at their worst, she hired a childhood friend as a bodyguard. Wherever she went, her friend and bodyguard went with her. He was a contract laborer, and didn't have much in the way of self-confidence. He was introverted and bad-tempered, letting fly at the drop of a hat and even getting into fights on a regular basis.

"Do you like living life this way?" Tang asked him one day.

"I don't like it, but there's nothing I can do about it," he said. "I can't control my feelings."

"So, what kind of life would you like to be living?"

"I'd like a life where I had my own car, and I could go places with my friends and hang out."

"If that's the kind of lifestyle you'd like, is there no way you can change?" Tang asked.

"I suppose if I can imagine it, maybe I can do it."

"If your life was really like that, do you think you'd still be getting into fights?"

He started to explain all the situations that led to him getting into fights, and they all amounted to things people said that he found personally offensive.

"Don't you get tired?" asked Tang. "You're never sure, from day to day, whether the things people are saying really mean something or not, but whatever they say you have to react to it – even lash out at them. Isn't that stupid? If somebody provokes you, you get angry; but when you think about it, that makes *you* the loser, and *you* end up the foolish one."

He laughed.

"If you were a bit cleverer," said Tang, "you'd be the one in control of your feelings. You wouldn't allow anyone else – at least not just with a few words – to be able to determine how you felt. If you want to change, you can start there, by being the master of your own emotions."

It was a turning point for Tang's bodyguard friend. He still lost his temper from time to time, but he started to become aware of what was happening when he did. Tang even began to tease him about it. "You're being stupid again," she would say, "but that's OK. Go ahead and be the loser."

Gradually Tang's friend became more aware of what he was doing. In the past, everyone had been afraid of him, afraid of rousing his temper. He was renowned as being impossible to communicate with, and as a result he had few friends. But through coaching techniques, Tang helped to settle him down. He started to learn to manage his emotions, and with it his communication skills started to improve. His confidence also slowly came back, and over time he began to make friends again. It also had an impact on his work. With his improved communication skills he found he could take on his own clients and projects. For him, this was an earth-shattering change, as if he had become a new person. In the past, he communicated with his fists and his feet, but now he was communicating with words. When he was ready to change and accept other possibilities, there was a complete readjustment in his life. Before, when he was buried in his emotions, it was as if he was blind and could see nothing.

"From being a scrappy laborer with an inferiority complex, to being a confident, calm, passionate, and communicative private entrepreneur, that's the kind of change that can take place with coaching," says Tang, a woman who brought a near moribund family business back to prosperity. 人

Chapter **5**

# REVOLUTIONIZING
## Retailing

I n January 2006, the Guidu Department Store in the northern Chinese city of Taiyuan was a hubbub of workshops and strategy meetings. Mobile phones were beeping in concert as military-themed text messages swarmed out at regular intervals to the store's staff. "Congratulations to team No. 7 for consistently getting Grade A results. Only 15 days left to January 28. How far away is the target of 88 million yuan? How far do the field commanders have to advance every day to ensure success?"

"Shout in the direction of headquarters, 'Victory belongs to us!'" went another message.

Taiyuan, the smoggy capital of Shanxi province, has a population of around 2.5 million. Something of a laggard in China's recent spectacular economic development, the landlocked province is known mostly as the country's northern coal belt, and is home to some of its biggest steel plants. A trickle of tourists make their way to the city, mostly for its nearby Buddhist grottoes and the walled town of Pingyao, which in the Ming (1368–1644) and Qing (1644–1911) dynasties was China's leading banking center. Few people, however, would think to go there for the shopping.

For the Guidu Department Store, this was long an ideal situation. A retail space of around 25,300 square meters, and employing more than 1,300 staff, it carried the usual array of products one would expect of a mid-level city anywhere – clothing featuring high on the list, accompanied by a host of other items ranging from sports gear to furniture and electrical products. The store was, in other words, a retailer that aimed to be all things to all people, and its staff were motivated by catch-cries often heard in China: "Love and cherish the customer"; "Achieve perfection"; and, "Put people at the heart of service." With an excellent location in the "old city" commercial district, Guidu had become one of the pillars of the Liuxiang shopping district.

In its day, the Guidu Department Store changed Taiyuan shoppers' ideas about what a department store should be. The sudden appearance of a relatively modern shopping space, complete with a small music forum with a key-tinkling pianist and even occasional performances by quartets, was a revelation to Taiyuan residents, whose previous shopping experiences had been defined by the drab, erratically stocked shopping centers that were once commonplace in China. After all, even until well into the 1980s, shopping in most of China was an experience marked by desultory service and environments that seemed designed to discourage people from lingering any longer than was absolutely necessary.

By the late 1990s, however, a shopping revolution was under way, and it was marching into every corner of China. The Guidu Department Store found itself facing an entirely different market situation from the glory days when it had a local monopoly on style and customer service. The store began to be troubled by internal staff and management issues, as a cut-throat, live-or-die market emerged in Taiyuan's foremost commercial district. Having once outshone all other contenders, Guidu was now scrambling to catch up with the competition. And in addition to local new arrivals, a slew of foreign-run department outfits were also vying for the purse-strings of Taiyuan's shoppers.

Meanwhile, as those external pressures mounted, Guidu was finding it increasingly difficult to get its internal affairs in order. The store's hardware had failed to keep pace with the times. Modern Taiyuan shoppers were beginning to have higher expectations of high-end shopping centers, and Guidu's outdated appearance began to have a direct impact on its sales, as the store's popularity plummeted. When the *Ren* Coaching team arrived at Guidu in early September 2005, their first impression was that the store's lighting was too dim, giving it a gloomy appearance. But on closer inspection, they identified a host of other problems. Taiyuan may not be Shanghai or Beijing, but local shoppers were becoming more discerning, and Guidu's interior looked like it belonged to another era.

##  RESTRUCTURING DILEMMA

Guidu's initial response had been to embark on a major program of management restructuring aimed at improving competitiveness. Unfortunately, the restructuring brought instability, making it very difficult to gel Guidu's new management into a cohesive team. Meanwhile, disagreements with suppliers were starting to have an impact on the store's reputation. Hit hard by diminished sales, Guidu began to delay paying its suppliers, which created ill will. This, in turn, led to delayed deliveries of new products, and some didn't make it on to the store's shelves at all. To make matters worse, the store was having problems guaranteeing the quality of its products. Customers were starting to shop elsewhere.

Department stores tend to be loosely structured businesses. It is not uncommon, for example, for the different sales desks to have little communication with one another – each going its own way, and taking responsibility for its own sales targets. Perhaps this is symptomatic of a poorly developed corporate culture, but in Guidu's case the situation was spiraling out of control. It seemed that no one had overall responsibility for what was happening – or took it to heart.

By the time the *Ren* Coaching team entered the scene, staff morale was at an all-time low, and there was a sense that time was slipping away. Despite all their efforts, attempts by the management to consolidate and regroup had mostly done more damage than good.

It was a problem that Guidu chairman, Wei Jianhua, felt particularly acutely.

"From the beginning," he says, "Guidu always had the ability to turn things around, but staff factors were the bottleneck. The dwindling sales in recent years had eaten into staff morale in a major way. So, when I began to think about how to sort it out, obviously the staff were at the top of my to-do list."

But for Wei, the question of just how to do this was the difficult part. He had always been a believer in staff training, but despite a stream of consultants having passed through the doors of Guidu, nothing seemed to have changed. "Their influence was momentary rather than lasting, and even though we spent a lot of money, after they left, there didn't seem to be any results."

##  FROM TRAINING TO COACHING

One of the major differences between coaching and training is that coaching emphasizes self-driven learning, and, more specifically, learning related to attitudes and beliefs. For Wei, his first encounter with this difference as a client himself was a revelation. Like many other senior managers in China who come across coaching for the first time, his first thought was how it might be incorporated into the workplace overall. The result was that the company's management teams began to enroll in the complete sessions of the *Ren* Coaching program.

For most of the management teams who undertook the program, this was the breakthrough they had been looking for. It was the tool they needed to overcome what Wei called the "staff bottleneck" – the basic conundrum that was holding back the business on every front.

"The difference between coaching and other methods is that coaching is focused every minute, from start to finish, on practical results," says one senior manager. "And when the courses are finished, there is a sense that the real learning is only just beginning."

He was referring to something that nearly every client who experiences the *Ren* Coaching Model tends to remark on. "There are a lot of things that you pick up in daily life, but what coaching gives you, you can use, put into practice, translate into something positive, and end up in a completely new place. Unconsciously, our behavior patterns are changing, and we're adopting new, positive behavior patterns. When the first group of us came into contact with coaching, we all felt that if we brought this set of skills into the workplace we could activate the staff's potential and break out of the deadlock we were in and move to a new level."

But adopting a coaching culture in a business doesn't happen overnight. In the early stages, many senior managers found themselves facing utterly new concepts, and many were skeptical about whether they could be applied or put to good use. Early advocates such as Wei Jianhua and several others, however, didn't let this put them off. Ignoring the nay-sayers, they organized supplemental classes for the more skeptical staff members and set about drumming up enthusiasm for further coaching courses.

According to Guidu's assistant manager, Li Hongyuan, Guidu had been doing things in half-measures. Although in the past the store had always done good business, it had never put as much effort into the business as it might, and had always balked at throwing resources at challenges. "I think at the time the morale of my team was at a low ebb," he says. "With the pressure on us to ascend to new heights, adjustments needed to be made to the team, and we started to look to coaching skills to help us achieve this. In the past, we had always relied on our own experience, the experience we had accumulated. When it came to new problems, we dealt with them the way we had dealt with the old ones."

 ## GOING THE FULL MILE

The *Ren* Coaching team's role, however, was not only limited to changing the way Guidu's staff thought and went about doing their work. Even before the full-scale courses got under way, the team began to scout out and research the main competitors in Guidu's vicinity, and came up with a series of suggestions for improving the store's appearance and the flow of funds. Senior management was closely involved, and made a snap decision to upgrade the store's outmoded interior. Meanwhile, suppliers were invited to meet with Guidu's management and make frank suggestions for improvements. The result, finally, was the recognition that there was an urgent need for better coordination of fund flows. At the heart of this decision was the acceptance that it was necessary to adopt a win-win mentality if the store was to win back the trust of suppliers frustrated by delayed payments.

The program didn't stop there. From September to mid-November 2005, Guidu and the *Ren* Coaching team joined forces to carry out a three-stage "human-capital program" of change aimed at drumming up the staff's sense of responsibility. Suppliers were also encouraged to participate: the objective – to encourage a harmonized, win-win atmosphere.

In September, 145 senior management and staff joined a team-building course that aimed to get to the bottom of the store's staff problems. The course set itself the mission of building mutual trust, effective communication, mutual support and better cooperation, so that everyone could start working together to reach shared goals.

## ▦ OVERCOMING DOUBTS

Taiyuan is a far cry from vibrant, relatively cosmopolitan Beijing or Shanghai. For most of the Guidu staff, modern management theories were like an alien faith – or a message from another planet. They were curious about the workshops, but took a wait-and-see attitude to their potential benefits. But for most, that was an attitude that quickly changed. Within two days of starting experiential workouts, most participants had completely embraced their new roles and started to implement the principles of coaching into their lives and work.

"Before entering this coaching course, I had my doubts," says one of the participants. "I didn't have any expectation that I would be affected by the course at all. But when yesterday's activities had come to an end, I realized I'd had a complete shift in my thinking. Here's a simple example – listening. Are you a good listener or not? I remember there were three points. One, you're not a good listener because you're tenaciously defensive of your own opinions. Two, you're not a good listener because you only want to hear your own opinions. Three, you're not a good listener because deep down you don't respect other people's opinions. In the past, I always thought I was someone who respected other people, but in actual fact that wasn't true. When I gave an opinion, I simply wanted approval from everyone around me, but when other people said something I rarely accepted it. Yesterday on the way home I kept asking myself, what kind of person am I? Am I good at listening or not? What exactly can I do to make myself better? I think, at that point, I had already started on the road to self-improvement."

This was no unique experience. Throughout what was once a very quiet work environment, staff were soon swapping stories of revelations they had had about themselves. For many, this first experience of coaching was a transforming one.

One participant excitedly summed up his feelings at the end of the course: "This coaching thing has allowed me to see the human, caring side of many of the managers. I'd never seen that before. But like everyone else, they have an honest, innocent side, and are full of potential. I think when we're working together we tend to overlook this, as if it's crushed in some way by the management system itself. Normally, we overlook the power of the team, emphasizing the power of leadership and downward pressure – orders from on high. Today I'm excited because I've seen a new team emerge that is completely different from the one I used to work with. This team is motivated, and full of energy, creativity, and passion; it's cooperative and capable of sweeping aside all obstacles."

Dinners held after the team-building workshops were marked by excited exchanges of opinions about what people had experienced during the day, and many wanted to know whether there would be further courses. The mood was festive, almost like on Chinese New Year's eve, with staff going off together afterwards to sing karaoke.

# PUTTING IT INTO PRACTICE

In mid-September, taking advantage of the new mood in the store, a Power of Coaching workshop was held for 37 participants, including senior management and major brand-name suppliers.

The purpose of a Power of Coaching course is to pass on basic coaching knowledge and skills, so that in future coaching-style leadership can be implemented in day-to-day business. The program involves disseminating a coaching culture that improves the quality and skills of the management, while simultaneously empowering the general staff.

Once the participants had grasped the essentials of coaching, it was time to put their knowledge and skills into practice in the workplace. A 22-day implementation plan was got under way. Working behind the scenes were three *Ren* coaches and the deputy chief coach, Wu Yong-yi. Their mission was to help the participants use coaching principles to break the company's sales record for the National Day Golden Week holidays, in the first week of October. Using scheduled phone calls and short text messages, the team set about changing mindsets and increasing motivation to achieve its objectives. The process was well received by most of the staff, although some doubted that they were up to the challenge. But even at its most difficult moments, most of the staff realized they were on a journey that would see them grow as people.

## IDEALS AND GOALS

A Guidu supplier of eight years standing said of the experience: "I realized that coaching is a powerful set of battle strategies. From the moment I encountered them, I started to use them with my staff. And while doing this, I kept talking to the coaches about problems I was having to deal with. How could I get the staff to accept this newfound passion of mine, and make them as enthusiastic as I was? All the questions I had thrown at me really began to wake me up. Had we really ever established common team objectives and goals? Before National Day rolled around, we called a staff meeting. The topic was life ideals and goals. You know, a lot of people, once they get out of school, don't give a second thought to ideals and goals, but in this meeting everyone's expressions were rapt. All of them, I could see, had a strong will to improve themselves, and in fact they all had ideals and goals – it was just that they had never spoken honestly about them before. I asked whether there was a contradiction between having a good life and working hard. Most people had an opinion on this, and we reached a consensus. It was an amazing experience. You could sense the strength of the team growing, and I began to feel that I had a responsibility to provide a platform for everyone's ideals.

"The results of that meeting were way beyond my expectations. In the past, it was me who set all the goals – imposed them on the team – but this time they came up with their own goals, and they were much more challenging than anything I could have expected. And here's the thing, once they'd set those targets, their work also improved, producing real results. Our department's sales increased 13% on the previous year. After the National Day Golden Week holidays, we had another meeting. We'd allocated an hour, but it ended up lasting three hours. The reason: I gave everyone a questionnaire entitled 'Golden Week Experiential Study Report.' One demand the report made was that everyone present discuss the questions, and that every team come up with three points of view. What they came up with was amazing. I couldn't quite believe that in such a short space of time they had acquired a mindset for self-betterment and self-examination. They told me that in the past seven days they felt like they had competed in an intense sporting event."

Prior to the first *Ren* Coaching session, around 54% of the participants had completed a declaration of their goals, but after the second session of courses, held in the latter half of September, around 86% of the staff had identified their goals. During the Golden Week holidays, Guidu finally reversed the slide in sales that it had seen for two years running, providing a major boost to staff morale. And morale was boosted even further when, on the seventh and last day of the holiday week, sales not only shot up 24% on the previous year but marked the third-biggest day of trading in the store's history. Everyone began to sense that the store had finally broken through what in the past had seemed to be an inherent law that sales dropped on holidays.

The staff began to talk about having a feeling of purpose and passion. The team was finally pulling together, and anything seemed possible. They were finding new methods and more effective ways of getting things done, and were learning to focus on their goals, to give praise before criticism, and to take responsibility for their own commitments.

Guidu had never carried out much in the way of appraisals of its own operations. Perhaps once a week, or every ten days, an order would come down from on high, but there was often no real objective, and the efforts were generally desultory. But after the coaching team set up shop in the store, that began to change. There was a new workplace rhythm, and efficiency improved. Periodic, and even daily, reports of results started to become the norm, and by the last day of the program teams were making hourly progress reports. This increased the target orientation and motivation of the teams enormously.

"We began to conclude that the coaching plan was actually compelling people to success," says Guidu's general manager, Wang Hongqi. 人

# Chapter 6

# From
# MANAGEMENT to
# LEADERSHIP

Business meetings in China tend to follow a typical pattern: the boss speaks and the staff listen. After all, it is the boss's company, the boss who rose to the top, and it is the role of the staff to listen and imitate. In essence, the corporate cultures of most Chinese companies are whatever culture the boss puts in place. Taiwanese companies – and tens of thousands of them run assembly lines in China – are often perceived as even more extreme. Management structures are almost military in style, with the boss exerting power rather like an all-powerful general. Staff hierarchies are strictly defined and, in the daily running of business, there is a tendency toward bureaucratic inflexibility.

Yang Ming-kung, the chairman and general manager of Taiwan's Huabao Electronics, was one of those bosses who ruled inflexibly from the top down, and his company had the classic Taiwanese hierarchical structure. But, as his staff grew to 1,200 from the company's small beginnings in 1997, and Huabao's annual turnover on 10 varieties of electronic goods – mostly computer and mobile phone components – reached US$50 million, Yang began to find it increasingly difficult to maintain his grip on the business's concerns.

"One in three computer USBs and digital camera fire wires are produced by Huabao," says Yang. "Big companies like Sony, NEC, Canon, Apple, and Logitech are all our customers. Logitech alone needs around 10 million connectors a month and we supply all of them."

Yang worried that he was driving himself into the ground by trying to micro-manage the business and personally taking responsibility for every decision that needed to be made in the company.

The turnaround came in 2003, when Yang visited a friend and business associate in Hong Kong. The first thing that struck him on that visit was the attitude of his friend's staff – they were friendly, efficient, and engaged with what they were doing – and it occurred to him that he was in a company with an excellent corporate culture.

But then he noticed something else as well. While talking with his friend, it occurred to Yang that he was in conversation with a man who was in control but still seemed relaxed. Yang wondered, "Am I working too hard?" He began to ask his friend questions about his business and learned that 35 of the company's senior staff had recently undertaken *Ren* Coaching program in Guangzhou. His curiosity piqued, in November of that year, Yang signed up too.

##  SHIFTING A MINDSET

"In 20 years as an entrepreneur, I had always subscribed to the old saying, 'It's about issues, not people,' says Yang. "But as my business grew bigger and bigger, there were more and more of those issues, and everybody got increasingly tired. And it was purely by chance – that meeting with a friend. He was so carefree and relaxed, the envy of everyone who knows him, and he told me that the *Ren* Coaching program had been a big influence. It immediately got me to thinking about whether I could achieve his air of calm achievement, and what these coaching programs were about."

For Yang, the results were close to instant. No sooner had he completed the courses than he enrolled his management. As they completed the courses, communication between managerial departments started to become much smoother and the improved atmosphere of responsibility soon resulted in greater efficiency.

The issues that had been piling up for so long without being resolved started to melt away, Yang recalls. "It was a situation I never could have imagined in the past."

"I'd been in business for 20 years when I came to China in 1997," says Yang. "I was always tired, because I was the only one giving orders. Everything had to come from 'Chairman Yang,' and as a result I was exhausted day and night. In the past I was always dressing people down about things that weren't working out the way I wanted them to. My staff saw me as the bad guy, and as my business grew year by year so did my temper. My business was growing, but I wasn't."

Yang recalls being tested for a local driving license shortly after he brought his production to Dongguan, Guangdong province's sprawling industrial belt, in 1997. He was driving in fourth gear, and the tester suddenly said to him in a thick southern brogue, "Change into third." Not having a clue what the man had just said, Yang continued driving in fourth gear. The tester repeated himself, "Change into third," and added: "Do you understand what I'm saying?"

Yang says he laughed aloud.

"What's so funny about saying, 'Change into third'?" the tester asked.

"It's that phrase," Yang tried to explain to him. "You know, 'Do you understand what I'm saying?' I say it myself every day. I've been saying it for years now to my staff."

Later, after he changed the way he interacted with his staff at work, Yang realized that the question was a cornerstone of his management style. For years, he had taken on the responsibility of personally teaching his staff everything he thought they should know, and after imparting something to them he would ask, "Do you understand what I'm saying?" If they said, "Yes," he had them repeat it back to him word for word.

##  INSPIRED BY THE COACH

"While I was in the first *Ren* Coaching course," says Yang, "I watched a coach dealing with a client's problem with perfect poise. It immediately struck me that it would be amazing to be able to handle problems at work like that, and it made me an instant convert to the coaching culture. By February of the next year, I was already using the techniques I'd learned with my employees. It was a major shift. In the old days, things only happened when 'Chairman Yang' opened his mouth. Suddenly my staff were opening their mouths and making things happen."

It was a change with far-reaching implications. "In the early days of the business," says Yang, "all the company's objectives were my objectives." The problem was, the staff often couldn't meet the objectives Yang had set. And the reason was very simple, though he couldn't see it at the time: the demands were his and not theirs. "It's not like that any more. Nowadays in meetings I ask the staff, 'What do you hope for in the future? How can you meet your objectives? What do you think the time frame will be?' They make their own plans, and this has produced a very different corporate culture."

Yang's management style has undergone a major shift, according to a member of his management team who has worked with him for years. "He's now more willing to accept different kinds of people. His communication method has changed. In the past, everything had to be carried out according to the boss's policy, and when it was time to sit down and talk with him there was an enormous pressure. Now he's open to other people's opinions, and you can go into meetings with him feeling much more relaxed."

The traditional management approach of placing all authority in the hands of a company boss or a small management team has no place in an organization that has embraced a coaching culture. The *Ren* Coaching Model teaches that responsibility is a two-way street. Leaders have to offer their staff the opportunity to make contributions if they want them to shoulder responsibilities. They also have to assess situations in consultation with staff and then delegate responsibility for dealing with those situations to those who can do it best.

## SUPPORTING GROWTH

One of Yang's sons undertook the *Ren* Coaching program. Afterwards he asked his father, "Dad, what would you like me to be in future?"

Yang thought for a moment, wondering how a coach would answer such a question. Then he replied: "What would *you* like to be? What are your hopes for the future? You figure that out, and I'll do everything I can to work with you on them."

For what can only be described as selfish reasons, we often overlook a powerful facility we have – the ability to listen. Far too often, we forget that listening is learning. For Yang, the change from barking orders at his staff to encouraging them to speak out, from cussing them to asking them questions and listening to their answers, was a profound shift. Yang had put aside his authority as the boss and opened a space for his staff to develop themselves. He was no longer the man with all the answers, and suddenly it was his staff who were the source of energy and inspiration. These are changes that go to the heart of what fostering a coaching culture is all about: in all business matters, the vitality of an organization comes from its people. And each of those people has their own desires, knowledge, and ways of thinking. If they are not motivated to grow as people, then the organization cannot grow either.

From a coaching perspective, Yang made the transition from being a manager to being a coaching-style leader. The distinction between management and leadership has been hotly debated in the business world, but in a coaching culture it is simply that managers concern themselves with how to get things done, while leaders concern themselves with how things influence people. While both are equally important roles, when a manager makes the transition to a leadership role, as Yang did, it can be compared to making the transition from competence to excellence.

 ## THE NURTURING PATH

Yang Ming-kung was the eldest of five children. He had a hard-scrabble childhood, joining the workforce at the age of 14, after finishing elementary school. He took an apprenticeship in a metalworking factory, and at the age of 26 he founded his own business. More than three decades on, Yang admits that for most of his life as an entrepreneur he had "no idea what management was all about."

"I was a homegrown metalworker, and I was scared to hire people who were any good," he recalls. "The people I hired were people I had confidence in, and the only people I had confidence in were people with similar backgrounds to myself – they had to speak my language. These days I have a lot of people working for me that I would never have hired before. Coaching has helped me to differentiate between people's personalities and their skills. For work-related skills I use training methods. When it comes to people's attitudes, I use coaching methods."

Like many of his compatriots from prosperous Taiwan – which has been developing for decades – when he came to China, Yang says he unconsciously had a sense of superiority toward the mainland Chinese. When he mixed with locals in Dongguan, he had a high-handed attitude toward them. "The first *Ren* Coaching course I did changed that. None of us knew each other, but within four days we were communicating as if we were old friends. We're still in touch today. Like the rest of the group, I lost my sense of distance from the others. And when I went back to work, I started to feel the same way with my local staff. It completely changed my outlook, and I began to realize just how much local talent there was in China."

But the change also affected the way Yang communicated with staff that had come with him from Taiwan. In the past he had problems communicating his feelings, even with people he had worked with for many years. It frustrated him, for example, when people came to him with problems they might easily have fixed themselves. And at other times he found it difficult to correct staff when he knew they had taken a wrong decision. The turning point, he recalls, was during an advanced private coaching session.

"If one of your deputies is doing things inappropriately, is that because it's how you have taught him to do it?" asked the coach. "By watching him take the wrong path and not pulling him up on it, have you ever wondered whether you're encouraging him to continue on that path?"

"It was a moment in which I suddenly woke up," says Yang. "It's true that by seeing something and doing nothing about it, I was effectively tacitly agreeing to it. I decided it was time for me to start being more direct in the workplace, to speak out about my ideas, and to pay attention to the things that needed my attention."

Yang had broken through a blind spot. The only problem was that the new Yang initially simply confused his employees – they couldn't understand his changed way of doing things. But after more than 20 management staff undertook the coaching workshops, the business began to develop the foundations of a coaching culture. Staff began to learn from themselves, and to question why they couldn't do certain things; it was a far cry from the days when admitting to performance problems would have been to invite the scrutiny of the boss. Today, the Huabao office meeting room walls are covered with Post-It notes and reminders about the coaching culture everyone is trying to instill in the company.

Yang has continued with the *Ren* Coaching program and has also volunteered as an assistant coach himself – an experience he has been able to incorporate into his leadership style.

"At work, we have a morning meeting. I probably attend it once or twice a week. After it closes, I use coaching techniques to do a summing up. I ask everyone what the situation is, what we need to be paying attention to, and what we've learned. In the past there was no summing up. One of the positive things about having been an assistant coach is that everything proceeds in a fixed direction toward the summing up, and I now use the same technique at work. In the past, employees left meetings with no fixed direction, walking out of the door as if nothing had happened. Now section heads provide everyone with a direction."

 ## REFORM AND EVOLVE

For Yang, the changes in the workplace haven't just been about the way he interacts with his staff but also about the way his business is structured, and he has gone about making radical reforms, not just once but three times. "I continue to become more aware of what I want," he says. "In the past, I was the chairman, and beneath me was a vice-chairman. Beneath him was our operations chief, and beneath him we had a general manager. And so it went, all the way down through the company."

Yang decided, as he puts it, to "flatten out" the old structure of the company, and do away with most of the division and section heads that stretched down to the lowest echelons of the business, placing a strategic planning committee beneath the general manager. What is more, he decided it was time to merge all the various sections that previously governed different lines of work into a single production section, so that all parts of the production process were communicating with each other.

"So, who is the section head of this new overarching unit?" Yang asks, with a look of self-satisfaction that he obviously cannot quite restrain. "Obviously there had to be one. Well, I decided, let them choose for themselves. I used the process that I had seen at work in the *Ren* Coaching program of allowing students to choose for themselves who will be their leader.

"In the advanced coaching courses," says Yang, "I learned to take a far more distanced view of things, and to try and survey a situation as objectively as possible. I'm trying to encourage the staff to learn, by asking them: 'How can we look at this in fresh ways?'"

The boss who at one time had all the answers says his policy today is to encourage staff to reflect on the fact that the road that brought them to their current place isn't necessarily the road forward. "We have to think about how we got here, because if we don't we have no way of figuring out how to achieve the goals we set ourselves for the year ahead. If we're here now and we have problems, we have to figure out how to turn them around, and that might mean a change of strategy. I'm encouraging everyone to think more, to exercise their brains. The more we do that, the more options are open to us, and the more progress everyone makes. The alternative is, we just mark time and keep walking the same old road."

The results have been tangible. Huabao's staff, according to Yang, are thinking more clearly, and are more willing to pull their weight. The tendency – which bedeviled daily operations in the past – to shift responsibility in the face of difficulties has been replaced by a sense of common purpose and open communication. "Coaching," says Yang, "has provided staff with a common language. I basically don't have to run the show anymore. I've given everything over to the staff. Sure, I take responsibility for important policy decisions, but the rest is theirs to handle."

There has been a similar revolution in the way Yang perceives his clients. In the past, he says, he didn't have a clear vision of what a win-win situation was, but after experiencing coaching he began to put himself "in the shoes of the clients" and think about what *they* wanted. "When I do an opening demonstration for clients, I know what it is they want. Above all, they want quality, and so that's what I show them – it's basic marketing psychology."

The other aspect of client relations Yang began to work on was service. He realized that a prevailing problem in the China market was that too often companies simply aimed to get their product into the hands of the customer. Once the customer had it, the product was theirs – for good or for bad – and if something went wrong or the production line didn't meet their expectations, the problem was theirs, too. Yang implemented a policy of "taking service to the home."

"If you're having problems with your production line, I can send technicians to your company to provide technical advice and sort out the problem. My customers, after all, are not end-customers. They have to sell on to clients of their own, and parts of their products are produced by me."

Yang picks up a short length of cable attached to a plug. "Take this. The plug is produced by me. What my client sells is the entire cable. If they're having trouble manufacturing it, they don't make any money – and nor do I. So today I take service all the way to my clients' production lines. But it's not something that ever occurred to me to do before."

##  THE PERSONAL TOUCH

For Yang, coaching hasn't just brought about a revolution in the way he does business; it's changed his life. "I bump into a lot of people these days who say, 'You're looking healthy and relaxed.' I always say to them, 'It's simple. I went to school.' I explain to them what kind of school I went to, what kind of courses I took, and I tell them how those courses helped me to grow. I hear constantly that I look energized again, unlike the old me, who apparently looked worn out, ground down. Well, I tell them, that's because most of my work nowadays is handled by other people. I'm occasionally asked how I could let go of control. I say, 'I learned about reverse thinking when I encountered coaching.' 'What's reverse thinking?' they ask. I explain: 'In the past I told everyone what to do. Now, I ask them how they want to do it.'"

Huabao's business grew by 26% in 2004, and now Yang has his sights set on a public listing by 2008. After that, he says, he wants to hand over the business to his team.

"I want to make the leap into consulting and coaching. It's something I would never have imagined before. But then, in the past, I didn't even dare to use people who were more capable than myself. Now I'm not afraid to use anyone. I didn't really know what to do with talent before. I had issues with whether I would be able to keep talented people if I hired them, but I realize now that that was simply about my own personal confidence. I've moved on from that. I've had a shift of mindset, and I know now that there's no one you cannot work with."

# Chapter 7

# Going to the
# MOUNTAIN

T ong Jie is a calming presence. He speaks softly, with quiet deliberation, as he reflects back on a life that has seen him graduate from the National Chinese Youth Table Tennis Team to being a business leader in China's shoe industry. He played table tennis from the age of six, but was forced out of the game at 18 by an injury. In need of work, the Beijing native headed south to Guangzhou, where – in the early 1990s – business opportunities were richer than in the north.

In Guangzhou, Tong joined a small shoe manufacturing firm and began to work his way up slowly through the ranks. It was an experience that taught him a lot about the industry. A labor-intensive business, it has developed arm-in-arm with a changing global labor market. In the 1950s and 1960s, the center of the shoe industry was Italy, but by the 1970s it was shifting to Japan and South Korea. The 1980s saw the emergence of Taiwan as the dominant player, and by the 1990s Taiwan was shifting production to the world's factory – Dongguan in Guangdong province. Today, China produces some 60% of the world's shoes, and increasingly China's shoe manufacturers have been moving toward designing and manufacturing their own brands. The vast majority of these, however, are shipped to discounted domestic stores to cater for growing local demand for inexpensive brands, despite the fact the market for name brands has been growing at a similar pace. The result: Chinese shoe shops are stocked with a huge array of brands, but the ones with hefty price tags are all imports.

It didn't take Tong long to see this, or to realize that the shoe industry could be divided broadly into three competitive layers. High-end imports came mostly from Italy and Spain, and other European countries. Mid-range imports came mostly from Hong Kong and Taiwan; while local Chinese manufacturers tended to fight it out for a slice of the bargain-basement market. Meanwhile, Tong also began to suspect that domestic manufacturers were ignoring product research and development at their own risk. If they were only in the business of processing materials for international orders or copying international brand names, it was unlikely they would ever progress up the value chain. To make it worse, as far as Tong could see, no one was carrying out any analysis of market demand. He began to feel that domestic manufacturers were heading for a bottle-neck – and fast. Unfortunately, his bosses didn't see it that way; they ignored his frequent recommendations for a re-think of direction and a new business model.

Tong's personal breakthrough came when he was introduced to coaching by a friend in an advertising agency. Coaching was a new concept for Tong, and he didn't have a clear idea of what it entailed or what it might do for him. But he was struck by the fact that his friend had clearly undergone some positive changes through his experience, so he signed up. After going from one course to more advanced courses in rapid succession, Tong began to feel that he could be doing a lot more than he was in his professional life, and in personal sessions with a coach his real goal started to become increasingly clear to him.

"I decided it was time for a personal breakthrough, to realize the ideas I'd had for some time," he says. "I decided to go my own way in business, and it was a decision that I owe coaching a lot for."

Tong saw the shoe industry as being divided into upstream and downstream elements. Upstream were the factories, and downstream were the outlets. The operators who worked the middle ground tended to be inefficient, and so this was the area that Tong decided to stake out for himself. His idea was simple: to create a brand through packaging while having someone else manufacture the product. Tong's company would be a kind of shoe marketing consultancy, bridging the gap between China's manufacturers and sales outlets.

"We let go of the idea of going into manufacturing, and decided instead to connect manufacturers and sales outlets to create a brand. Bringing a completely new local brand into being requires a massive investment, which is why no new brands had appeared in several years. I looked at the upstream factories and the downstream stores and realized that all that was needed to connect those two elements was good business skills. I was particularly interested in the successful model provided by McDonald's and KFC, and it seemed strange to me that the same principles weren't being applied in other industries. At the same time, I read everything I could on how to package a product, how to set prices, develop a brand, and so on, because it was clear to me that the value of these things couldn't be overemphasized. If you take two identical products and you put one of them through our packaging and our branding, its value leaps."

The goal that Tong acquired through coaching became the Mosilei Shoe chain. Although it doesn't operate its own stores, there are now more than 120 Mosilei-branded shoe outlets scattered throughout China. It also doesn't operate its own factories, and yet more than 3,000 people are involved in the production of Mosilei shoes. From a start-up investment of 5 million yuan (US$623,000), in the space of just two years Mosilei achieved annual sales of more than 100 million yuan (US$12.5 million).

"There are plenty of examples of successes in this business – especially when it comes to the established brands – but when you think about how we've come from nowhere to where we are today you could say that we're the best," says Tong. "There's a definite relationship between our growth and our business model. We've established a model for getting a brand off the ground. And we've learned how to do that through trial and error. We're not selling shoes, we're selling business skills."

## 卐 EACH ACCORDING TO HIS ABILITY

"Before I got involved in coaching," says Tong, "whenever I looked at a problem, I looked at it from a very personal perspective. The biggest reward I got out of coaching was that I felt as if, all of a sudden, I had matured immensely. I could look at problems from multiple perspectives, and suddenly I had the ability to see the bigger picture. In the past, I was forever splitting hairs and was too focused on details. Now I'm better at discovering new possibilities. I discovered that, as a team player, there were actually many things I could be doing that I wasn't. It was a discovery that really shook me, like a sudden awakening."

As a former sportsman, Tong had always taken coaching for granted; it was an essential element in striving for excellence as a table-tennis player. However, it was a revelation when he realized that coaching could also be applied to life and business. But his experience of sports coaching has also given him his own perspective on coaching in the workplace.

"When I was a sportsman," says Tong, "I always felt that you had to look at the caliber of the material you were dealing with. By that, I mean, if you're coaching someone for excellence, you shouldn't be blindly encouraging them to improve. If you want to raise their game, you need to look hard at the person and think about what they're capable of. I often see people who have experienced coaching leaping into coaching others and not discriminating carefully enough about what is right and wrong for the clients. For me, if you can't figure out what the person's current situation is, don't go ahead and start coaching them."

Coaching in the workplace is like sports coaching, says Tong, because before encouragement can be used to impel someone to greater efforts and more success, they have to have the skills they need to achieve that success. "In sports, a lot of skills have to be practiced repeatedly – practice makes perfect." Tong admits that encouragement can be an extremely useful tool, whether for sports players or for corporate executives, but only when they have acquired the skills they need.

"If you think about sports, when you get to a certain level, the competitors' levels of skill are pretty much the same, but the results they get in a competition can differ enormously. That difference is due to attitude – champions have a champion's attitude. That's very important. A lot of high-level sporting competitions are actually psychological competitions – it's two psychologies that are fighting it out, because it's your psychology that determines the level of your game."

 ## COACHING THE SELF

Tong has discovered that the best way to achieve that attitude of success is to use the principles he has learned in coaching on himself. That has meant recognizing his own strengths and weaknesses and then working on them. He says, for example, he has learned to keep a distance from many of the business's day-to-day issues, because he feels he has a tendency to compromise too easily and to see things from the position of whoever he is negotiating with. He now concentrates on devising strategies for building the company he founded, which is something he says he should be doing anyway, and also happens to be good at.

On the issue of coaching other people, however, Tong is wary. "I looked at it," he says, "and I could see immediately that it would be a very difficult thing to do. The main problem is understanding what the other person's situation really is. There is simply too much that you can't know. And if you don't know someone's situation, then you're blindly coaching them. I'm not sure that's a good thing, and it might even have results that are the opposite of those you were looking to achieve."

Tong calls self-coaching, a process of "adjustment." He says it is necessary to be constantly adjusting ourselves to our external circumstances. "It's like that old saying, 'The mountain won't come to me, so I'll go to the mountain.' In the past, I used to be overcome with negative emotions whenever things turned bad, but now I concentrate on coaching myself through it and adjusting myself to whatever's happening around me. And I try to do the same thing when things are going really well. I don't allow myself to gloat when everything seems to be going just the way it should. I think this process of self-adjustment is something you can take with you wherever you go – it's always present. In a way, it's a reminder that maintaining a normal emotional state isn't easy."

Frequent setbacks are an inevitability for anyone doing business, Tong says, but he feels the important thing isn't the setbacks themselves but our own outlooks, and how we react to events. He calls self-coaching "a process of adjusting our outlooks and reactions" to those setbacks.

"In China today, if you want to set up a large-scale enterprise, you've got to be prepared to face a lot of challenges because this is a society in such rapid transition. It's changing so fast, you need a new hand of cards every three years. Even a business like mine, which is still very young, has had a huge number of setbacks. You work hard to get the thing growing, but once it starts growing at the speed you want it to, contradictions start to emerge. The most typical one is that your human resources cannot keep up, and that's a huge problem. We've got a very simple business model, and it's a model that can be reproduced on a large scale, but human talent isn't something that can be reproduced on a large scale at the drop of a hat."

Self-coaching, says Tong, is a way of becoming more aware of the real problems that stand in the way of expanding a business to a large scale. "We have to know where we are in the business. At every stage of development a business has its objective rules. There are always times when colleagues could be doing really well, but due to some outside influences, or subjective reasons, they end up making a mess of things. At moments like this, our instinct is to give them a dressing down, to criticize them. After coming into contact with coaching, I learned to adjust my own thinking, and to stand in their shoes for a moment. What went wrong, and to what extent am I responsible? Actually, no one wants to make a mess of things, and when they do they feel enormous pressure – so much so that they may even be afraid of seeing you. So, the more someone is doing badly, the more they deserve your concern."

That concern, however, in Tong's view, should translate into assistance, not simply pity, because too much concern can also be debilitating for a distressed staff member. Staff who are doing well can best rally behind those who are falling behind by providing gentle reminders not to be too proud and to reach out for assistance whenever they need it. "What they are lacking isn't really concern – they're probably getting enough of that. They need some cool reminders of where they're going wrong, to help them relax a little."

## LEARNING TO LEAD

Too many Chinese business leaders, says Tong, have an attitude that it is the employees who need to be learning, not themselves. But, if the leadership isn't prepared to learn, how can it lead the employees to learn? Tong recalls an experiential exercise he participated in one time, in which a roomful of people were split into two groups, and everyone apart from the two leaders of the groups was blindfolded. The task for the leaders was to lead their groups along a meandering path to a designated destination.

"For me," says Tong, "that's how a lot of business leaders go about running their businesses. The staff at lower levels have no idea where the boss is taking the business – he or she is the only one who is possibly clear about that – and everyone else is just blindly following. But for a team to have cohesion and be efficient, both the leadership and the key people running the company need to be both ready to learn and in communication about where the business is heading. As a managing director, I think the first step in doing that is to coach myself."

 ## THE QUEST FOR TALENT

Tong attributes to coaching his enhanced ability to trust others and see their strengths. He discovered that when he genuinely let go and allowed other people to act for themselves, things got done, and the business grew more smoothly. "When you're trying to do everything yourself, you're inevitably going to make a lot of mistakes. But when other people make mistakes, it's usually the case that we don't forgive them, and come to the conclusion that they're simply useless. When you think about it, though, how many mistakes have we made along the way? Why is it we can forgive ourselves and not forgive others?"

Still, he says, extending trust is something that has to be done with eyes wide open. "First of all, you have to know what your colleagues' strengths are, and not just blindly empower, encourage, and trust people. In our daily work, we can see that certain people have areas of expertise and particular strengths. The trick is putting the right person in the right place, and then encouraging them to act and to get things finished. We can offer people guidance while they are doing this, but the important thing is that they are aware that they can use their own methods to do things even better, while nurturing their courage to experiment. That's a coaching method, actually. At the moment, the business is growing extraordinarily fast, and I think the main reason for that is that I'm not afraid to trust people, not afraid to let them do things their own way, and allow them to make mistakes."

Tong had an assistant who was formerly responsible for corporate planning in another company. After she married and became pregnant, she gave up that job and spent two years house-bound. Initially, Tong hired her as an assistant to carry out light secretarial duties for him. But as he watched her work he realized she was extremely organized and very thorough – much more so than Tong was himself, in fact. As he began to wonder whether he should give her more responsibilities, he also began to notice that she had great communication skills.

"Because we're something of a business platform, with neither factories nor stores, communication is extremely important – it's essential to connecting our upstream and downstream clients. So we really need efficient colleagues with good communication skills – people who can understand the clients and their needs. When my assistant communicated with people, I could see that she was very good at seeing things from their positions. And she was also very objective. So, essentially she had everything she needed to be doing more – she simply lacked some practical skills. And with skills it's often only in the process of actually doing things that you can learn and internalize them, so I took a leap of faith and sent her to work in the Customer Service Department. That's a department where we usually put only very experienced staff, but I had a sense that she would pick it up very quickly. If I hadn't let her go, her development in the company might have been a slow process, but now, in the space of just two years, she's already a deputy general manager – in this business, I think that's some kind of record."

Another Mosilei employee started out in distribution – a key logistical aspect of a business that is connecting shoe manufacturers with stores scattered across China. While on the job, the employee became interested in brand image – in particular, with how the stores selling Mosilei shoes packaged themselves in terms of interior décor. "At the time," says Tong, "I was the only person in the company who was working on brand image, but this employee in distribution came to my attention. He had high standards, was meticulous, and was particularly good at organizing his time. It struck me that there were certain things about him that might make him suitable for the branding work I was doing, and I decided to give him a shot. I didn't give him any guidance in the beginning. I just put him on the front line to see whether he could put his ideas into practice. In the beginning, the pressure on him was intense, but he grew with the job very quickly, which proved to me that sometimes throwing people in the deep end is a good method. Within a year, he had matured so much that today I basically have nothing to do with the brand image of the company. There's actually nothing really I can tell him, because now he's basically more specialized in the field than I am, and his demands are greater than mine."

Tong has carried out the same policy in all key areas, seeking out the best people for the job and giving them full responsibility for their departments. The main part of the job for Tong has been to use coaching techniques to encourage his appointees – to talk to them about their plans for the coming year, and whether they might set themselves even higher goals. The result, says Tong, is that today he is a far more relaxed person than he was in the past.

"In the old days, I had to be in charge of everything – from big to small – and because of that, I was constantly exhausted. Even more, I discovered I simply couldn't do a good job, because I was trying to focus on too many things at the same time, and that in turn was holding the company back. I felt like we were stalled and unable to grow beyond a certain point. Coaching made me realize that the reality is, within the structure of a company, people in different positions have to deal with different issues. For me, the direction and strategy of the business is the important thing; if I can think through that, then the rest of it can be handled by other people. You've just got to become good at distinguishing outstanding qualities in others. Once you can do that, everything becomes much easier and the business takes care of itself. I realized it was all about accepting the innate differences in other people. Everyone has very real strengths, innate talents, ideas and ways of thinking. Promoting those is about allowing people to have the space to explore them. That was the transformation that came over me through coaching."

It is an ethos that, Tong says, has become central to Mosilei. "I think the key people in our organization are very clear about what our business model is. There's a consensus on key issues – what our core competitive strengths are and how we can win. It's also key that everyone in the company understands that they are growing with the company, and it's only if the company is doing well that they can develop themselves."

Chapter **8**

# Living out a
# PROPHESY

After graduating from university with a degree in finance, Liu Xiangxiu took a job in booming Shenzhen. In 2000, at just 30, she was a department manager at a finance holding company, and commanding a salary that many in Guangdong province's rags-to-riches, border boomtown could only dream of. There was just one slight problem; Liu was bored with her work. She frequently felt that she was simply on track to becoming a certified accountant, and she wasn't sure that was where she wanted to go with her life. After much thought, she finally decided there was no point in waiting until she was retired to start doing what she really wanted to do. She quit her job.

"At the time," says Liu, "my sister wanted to go overseas to study, but first she needed to transfer the ownership of a beauty salon she was running. The family talked about it and we decided, why not let me take over the shop, seeing as it was a line of work I was interested in."

The reality of running a beauty salon, however, wasn't at all like anything Liu had imagined. Despite the fact she had been running a department of her own at the financial holding company, she found her experience was practically useless when it came to running a salon. "We had employees who didn't talk to anyone because they had been bullied to the point of tears by other workers, and I could see that customers were deliberately avoiding the shop. The place was being run by people who basically didn't seem to understand the first thing about doing business."

And yet, in the space of five years, Liu had grown that small salon into a chain of salons which, along with her other business interests, employed more than a thousand employees. With her business growing at anywhere between 40% and 60% annually, she even finds the time to work as a coach.

 ## A CHANCE ENCOUNTER

By the end of her first year running the salon, Liu was depressed. The problems at the salon seemed to be intractable. So, when she heard from a customer that her boyfriend had attended a course that had brought about some big changes in his life, Liu decided to take a look for herself. As it happened, her curiosity coincided with a nearby seminar introduction to coaching, and after attending Liu found herself even more curious. The seminar had an electric energy that she had never encountered before – everyone seemed full of life, vigorous, and yet sophisticated and polite at the same time. The seminar was about how to find conviction, and was accompanied by short performances that illustrated the points made by the speakers. Liu sensed that she had blind spots that could be overcome, and signed up for the course.

The experiential coursework that she underwent in her first four-day coaching course had a profound impact on Liu. She had always described herself as a "relatively reserved person," and had had difficulty opening up to others ever since she was a child. The trust games, frank and personal interactions, and close contact she was required to have with strangers during the course were a shock to her. But it was a shock that brought about changes.

Liu's parents were divided on whether or not this was a good thing. Her mother was worried and suspicious when her daughter returned from the course filled with excitement. But her father said it sounded like an "education revolution" that could bring about real change for people who experienced it, and suggested that she continue with the program. Liu promptly enrolled for the program. When Liu had completed the courses, she convinced her sisters to join them, too.

 ## A REVERSAL OF FORTUNE

It was while she was in the practicum of *Ren* Coaching model that Liu began to see the real value of coaching. "I set myself a target to increase the salon's business volume by 50% within three months," she says. "At first I made the target 30%, but then I changed my mind and made it 50% because it occurred to me that maybe I was playing it too safe, and not setting myself a big enough challenge. It was also a decision, though, that filled me with fear, because I'd never been able to achieve anything close to that in the past. In the end, I needn't have worried because within one month business grew by 90%! It was a shock to everyone I knew. I don't think it had occurred to anyone that you could drum up so much business at a beauty salon. I began to realize that the salon couldn't just support me; it could also make money. I raised the employees' salaries, and all of a sudden it seemed as if everything was changing around me. Everyone could see it – my family, the staff, the customers."

Liu brought one of her aunts in to work at the salon, which brought the total number of employees to 12. It was still a small operation, and despite the improvements most of the staff doubted that it would be possible to sustain the rapid growth they had seen recently. "A sparrow may be small, but it's a fully formed life," Liu told her staff, quoting a Chinese saying. "We're going to become a chain of salons, and I want turnover to reach 500,000 yuan [US$62,250] a month."

Liu says she wasn't only trying to inspire her staff, enrolling them in her dream, but also awakening herself to possibilities. And now that those early goals have long been surpassed, she looks back wonderingly and says, "I feel like I'm living out my own prophesy."

 ## IT'S ALL ABOUT COMMUNICATION

The Liu family has four daughters, and under Liu's influence all of them joined the *Ren* Coaching program before joining her in the growing beauty salon business.

"The biggest influence has been in terms of communication," says Liu. "A lot of things can go wrong in a family business, and without communication, if there are not fights over money, there are always going to be different points of view about how to get things done. But after having experienced coaching, we have a shared language and a high level of understanding of one another. We can differentiate between emotions and real issues, and we communicate about issues, not about emotions. When we're in a meeting and setting a new direction, we can usually adjust ourselves very quickly. But, still, we're not a business family. My father was a Party employee, and the rest of us all worked in finance. We have no business sense, so there's a lot of pressure. If we hadn't been through coaching, there's a good chance the whole thing would have fallen apart long ago."

Each of the sisters has clearly defined job descriptions. Liu describes her eldest sister as "the pilot," saying that she is responsible for the basic direction of the business. "She's very giving and also very capable. We all respect her. She's responsible for all the major equipment in the chain stores. The second sister is our financial director. The third sister is our 'elder stateswoman.' She went into the beauty business before any of us, and has been a lecturer and is a technology expert, so she's the IT director. And as for me, I'm responsible for management and business operations. For example, if we're opening a new store, the first step is for all four of us to scout out a location. Our eldest sister takes care of interior decor, and I take care of recruiting staff. My third sister will be in charge of training, and when the staff's trained I manage them."

 ## "WHAT I KNOW, WHAT I DON'T KNOW"

At the end of 2002, Liu established a second salon, and soon after she acquired the right to act as agent for an American brand-name beauty product. Suddenly she was running two salons and selling a new product – or as the Chinese say, running with both legs.

Liu describes what she learned from opening the second shop as figuring out "what I know, and what I don't know." She adds, "I know I can run a team of a dozen or so people, but I wasn't sure if I could run a team of several dozen people, especially when they were working in two very different environments."

From the outset, problems abounded. Staff would resign at the drop of a hat, while others floundered when it came to providing the quality of service that Liu was looking for. Liu also increasingly began to feel that she wasn't structuring the business in the way she should, and that she wasn't adapting well as the business grew. Meanwhile, as she searched for guidance, she discovered that there was virtually nothing in print about management for the beauty market. She was on her own.

"Competition within the industry is fierce, and there's no one who's willing to share anything with you because they're all protecting their patches," says Liu. "As an outsider to the business, there was nothing I could do but take my own winding path. There were times I almost fell, and a lot of things happened I could never have predicted, but at least my sisters and I had all been through coaching, and we were able to encourage each other and offer support."

## STUDY AND SUCCEED

Although Liu could see the benefits of coaching, as a beginner, she had difficulty putting what she had learned into practice. For instance, she had a tendency to want things to happen quickly, but at the same time she had high standards, and this combination of demands was often difficult for her employees to meet. But, while participating in a *Ren* Coaching study group, Liu had some revelatory insights into herself. She realized that many of the problems she was facing in the beauty business were of her own making. Without even realizing it, she had been limiting her employees' self-development and holding back the development of her business. She decided to make some adjustments. On the one hand, she started to consider how her employees really felt, and it became clear to her that most people who quit didn't really want to walk away. The challenge, she began to understand, was to find ways that employees' personal goals could be achieved within the parameters of the business. On the other hand, she realized that coaching was really about supporting and encouraging her team to win, not about she herself winning. In a major change of tactics, Liu began to provide more opportunities to her staff, which would allow them to explore their potential on the job.

Liu recalls how one particular coaching session enlightened her. One of her employees was chronically shy, and always stood with her head bowed. Liu's inclination was always to prompt the woman with the words, "Raise your head." But the coach said to the woman with a smile, "I'm sure that if you raised your head a little, you'd look very beautiful," and the woman, seemingly without even thinking about it, lifted her head. Liu suddenly saw clearly just how much more powerful trust and encouragement were than putting pressure on people.

"In fact," says Liu, "I realized the problem was me. I was worrying too much about things, and always seeing myself as the boss. My employees were my employees, and it was impossible for me to see them as my equals. And at the same time, when it came to so-called coaching techniques, all I was doing was using the words. Once I had this realization, I found that I was communicating much more openly with my employees, and it was almost as if I hadn't really done anything, that it happened naturally. It was like a mysterious force."

As the business grew, Liu started sending her more senior staff to attend study courses. Some of the courses were specialized beauty industry courses, and others were for attitude training. Some staff joined outdoor team-building activities and innovative thinking workshops, and it all worked to help build a coaching culture within the business.

"Coaching is all about people," says Liu. "Employees are like guests in your home, and customers are like guests you take out, say, for dinner. We appreciate our staff, and our staff appreciate being part of the culture we've created. A lot of them, if they leave, they come back, and others who leave for good don't have a bad word to say about us, and stay in contact after they're gone. The coaching culture is all about individual employees. I always say to the staff, a business is a chessboard, and we're all chess pieces, including me. Once we're off the board we're whatever the chess piece happens to be made of – a piece of wood or stone – but while we're on the board we all have functions we can put into play. I've put a lot of thought into this chessboard, and I tell the staff, this company is willing to train you to become a boss, but you can only become a boss if you make demands of yourself."

Success in business comes through a willingness to learn. Liu knew that for her business to grow she couldn't rely on her three sisters alone; she was going to need more resources. Only if she put her employees on an equal platform could the business prosper, so it was necessary to spend money and energy on training. As the management core of the business attended more and more courses, they became more efficient and the service standards improved. Liu began to be able to spend time away from the workplace, and to leave the daily running of the business to her staff. Meanwhile, communication had improved immensely, and this was obvious in meetings. In the past, a manager would deliver a sermon and the staff would sit quietly and file out when the sermon was over. Now the staff were standing up and speaking their minds about how the business was going and what they personally hoped to achieve. As a result, the entire business was becoming more cohesive as the lines of communication opened up between the staff and management.

##  PUSHING THE LIMITS

Liu and her sisters began to look beyond Shenzhen, promoting voluntary chain stores across the country. (In this system, stores cooperate with each other to offer favorable conditions for distribution of products, and sometimes management advice and interior design.) Within a year, they had opened two new businesses, three franchised salons, and a number of voluntary chain stores. The salons took the novel approach of fusing the spa concept with Western and ancient Tibetan medical principles. Voluntary chain stores were opened in the northern city of Tianjin, the landlocked central city of Wuhan, in Yunnan province in China's remote southwest, and in the nearby sprawling industrial belt of Dongguan. At the same time, the business obtained the rights to distribute international name-brand products throughout China, and registered the Oriental Beauty trademark in Hong Kong.

"I can't say that we had completely integrated a coaching culture into the business at that stage, but because I continued to study coaching techniques while we were growing really quickly, the way we communicated with the staff and trained them brought the culture into the organization over time. Our employees all knew how to listen, how to make distinctions, and to ask questions. Everyone was used to the fact that, during meetings, I might say something like, 'I'm going to give you some feedback on that.'"

For Liu, the business became a virtuous circle. The better the business did, the more she wanted to give back to the staff and the industry. Her next step was to establish a national beauty industry consultancy to train beauty professionals. She could see that many people wanted to invest in the business but had no idea how to manage, and the result was countless failures and bankruptcies. The aim of the business was to set up an alliance of beauty salons that used a national system to minimize operational risks through consulting on operations management, cost accounting, and training.

"For me, coaching has been a wonderful thing," says Liu. "It's given me a chance to be part of the process of people changing their lives. It brings self-respect, and with that we start to respect others more. It brings a sense of calling to a team, and becomes the core of an organization. But it's not only about business, because it can become part of our lives, and have a huge impact on everything we're involved in, bringing vitality and happiness with it. For me, it's become far more than a tool I use with my employees and customers; it's become part of me – a vital part of my thinking and the way I associate with other people. I use it everywhere; I use it in the way I reflect on myself, adjust my behavior, and search for new possibilities.

"Basically, it's helped me to become a new person. I've got more tolerance than I had before, and I've stopped haggling and fussing over petty details in life. I've learned to give and extend trust and love, as well as to encourage and challenge people. It's brought me and my sisters closer together, and we now have excellent communication and trust, not to mention the overall improvements it's brought in communication with the rest of the family."

# Chapter 9

# Believing in
# COACHING

After close on 20 years spent operating an electronics components factory in Dongguan, Guangdong province, Taiwanese founder and chairman of Toproot Electronics Co., Liu Chiu-chieh, had a problem. With around 1,400 employees in four Dongguan factories, and an annual turnover of around 100 million yuan (US$12.5 million), growth had been sluggish for the past two decades.

"The business had been around for a long time," says Liu. "But there always seemed to be limits on our growth. Even when we put the staff through training programs and it was obvious they had improved, overall nothing seemed to get any better. Most years we grew only around 5%, and the best we could manage was 10%."

But in July 2004, one of Liu's clients told him about how his younger brother had undergone a major transformation after attending a *Ren* Coaching program. For some reason, Liu found himself extremely moved by the story, and the next day he enrolled himself. "I thought, I've got to try this course and see for myself how it could completely change a person's life."

 ## LEARNING BRINGS CHANGE

The power that the course had to do just that became clear to Liu as he completed first one, and then the whole series of the coaching program. "It had a big impact on me," he says. "I'd always been the kind of person who analyzes things. When I was listening to people, my brain would be working away, analyzing what they were saying. But after experiencing coaching, I began to realize that that was all interference. I also realized I had a lot of other kinds of interference. For example, when I was mixing with people, there were countless things I liked and disliked about them. I needed to frame everything, and I imposed my own standards on everything. But now that's changed. Before, it was always 'You're the boss, you're the chairman, and they are the employees.' There was a distance between us. Now they can sense that I'm a lot more attentive when I'm dealing with them, attentive in encouraging them, and the professional distance between us has disappeared. What's more, I've become much better at managing and showing my emotions. When the mood is right, I laugh with the staff. I couldn't do that before, because I thought that as the boss I always had to be above all that. I'm not like that now, and I'm happier for it."

After his personal experience of coaching, Liu started to think about introducing it into Toproot. Perhaps, he thought, it might help solve the problems that had dogged the company for so many years. In August 2004, a team of middle management were sent to participate in *Ren* Coaching workshops, while study workshops were also organized for the company headquarters in Dongguan. A large number of recommended books were distributed, and Liu himself attended discussion groups with the middle management and upwards on the books' contents.

The results came more quickly than even Liu himself had imagined. "The first and most important thing that happened was that the atmosphere of the office underwent a complete change. In the past, there was a lot of wasted energy. When it came to the division of responsibility, it was easy for people to pass the buck.

We had four factories and each had a general manager who was concerned with maintaining his own power and looking after his own interests. After bringing coaching into the business, everyone started to communicate more directly, and they seemed to become more willing to accept responsibility."

They were changes that had an immediate trickle-down effect. For Liu, it was as if two decades of apathy were sloughed off, and employees across the board started to make a transition to being communication-focused, which in turn resulted in increased production.

"Every worker's attitude changed," says Liu. "They were suddenly calling meetings with their work groups every morning before they started work, and the objective of those meetings was to establish what objectives they wanted to achieve that day. They were figuring out how they were going to do the things that needed to be done, and who was responsible for what. There were also discussions about how to encourage team members, and analysis of whether it was possible to make breakthroughs in any areas."

As far as Liu is concerned, coaching gets results. After two decades of sluggish growth, in 2005, the year after coaching was introduced into the company, production was up more than 38%, a vast improvement on the previous annual average increase of

5%, while profits were up eightfold. "Apart from the growth in production," says Liu, "we've cut costs across the board."

Meanwhile, the newfound collaborative spirit at Toproot inspired Liu to seek a solution to another problem that had been bedeviling his business for some years. It was a common problem for factories operating in the heavily industrialized Dongguan area. The electricity supply was unable to keep pace with industrial growth, resulting in rolling electricity stoppages that interrupted production lines. The solution Liu and his team came up with was to use generators for production processes that didn't require much electricity, and then to employ heavy-consumption production processes after 11:00 pm, when electricity was generally available and only a third the price of daylight supplies. "This year's electricity costs were down 25% compared to last year," says Liu. "In the past, when the electricity stopped, work stopped."

##  PEOPLE MATTER

"People matter" is a phrase that rolls easily off the tongue, but applying it to the workplace is another matter. Coaching is a skill that is all about people, and while Liu was undergoing coaching himself, he personally had an insight that changed his outlook on his employees. In experiential exercises with strangers from all walks of life, Liu suddenly began to think about the enormous unrealized potential he probably had in his own company. Even so, it took time for him to truly implement this insight into his daily dealings with staff.

After coaching was brought into Toproot, work teams began holding frequent meetings. Liu was sometimes forced to drop out of these meetings at the last minute, because of a surprise visit by a client or because bureaucratic issues had come up unexpectedly. But, unlike in the past, the group leaders would now confront Liu directly whenever this happened, explaining that his failure to attend meetings made the staff feel that they were being neglected. Liu understood that accepting such criticism was essential to establishing the open, communicative environment the company needed.

"It made me feel happy that they were telling me directly how they felt," says Liu. "They were sharing their feelings with me, and that was helping me to see my blind spots."

Like many other bosses who have undergone coaching, Liu had come to the realization that when his employees spoke directly with him it was an expression of trust. He began to change his working habits, and at the same time to reorganize his commitments. "Now, it's the employees who come first, clients second, and investors third."

## SHARING THE PROFITS

Another major change at Toproot was the introduction of Key Performance Indicators (KPIs) as part of a new profit-sharing scheme for employees. It was a move, Liu says, that gave a major boost to morale. On the one hand, he says, coaching helped employees throughout the company to have a better sense of their goals and where they were headed; on the other hand, their boosted productivity was earning them more money.

And it was a move that made a big difference in recruiting and keeping employees. From 2002, factories in the southern coastal provinces of Guangdong and Fujian began to experience difficulties in attracting labor, as increasing numbers of rural migrant workers began to head north to the magnet of Shanghai, or stayed home as opportunities improved in the rural hinterland. For many of the factories that were having problems both recruiting and hanging on to their workers, the phenomenon was as problematic as the electricity shortages that were plaguing the region. But, for the new-look Toproot, these were no longer problems.

"Since bringing coaching into the company, our turnover rate for employees has been really, really low," says Liu. In the past, during the months of January to March – China's New Year period, when annual bonuses are paid out – Toproot, like other Dongguan businesses, would see a large number of staff resignations. In 2005, however, after Chinese New Year, only two out of the 1,400 employees resigned, while praise from its employees made it no problem for Toproot to recruit new staff. This was in contrast to many neighboring factories that were suffering from labor shortages. For Liu, it was a direct result of publicizing the business's KPIs and sharing profits with the employees.

"The staff are all saying that it makes them feel like they are entrepreneurs themselves, and they are keeping their eyes open for areas where costs can be saved. When all the employees are worrying about things like this, it's a very powerful force. As the chairman, you can only see so much yourself, but as a team the force is so much greater."

From a coaching perspective, any business leader should be able to answer the following questions: "What are the employees thinking? What do they want? What needs to be done if employees are to be motivated and creative?" As the Chinese economist Zhang Ruimin has said, "Human talent is a basic superiority in entrepreneurial competition. People can understand things, create things. All that is needed is the conditions, and they can adapt and change and become an inexhaustible resource."

# GO FOR BROKE

Liu has been running his four electronics components factories for a long time now and has rich experience in the field. The business has grown steadily over the years, but, he says, for some time his senior management have complained that electronics components is a fading industry, which puts real limits on growth. It wasn't until they had experienced coaching that he and others began to realize this was little more than an excuse. "We were holding ourselves back," says Liu. In fact, partly because it has been around so long, Toproot is among the top five names involved in the indirect export of electronic components. But despite this, it accounts for only around 8% of the total global market. When this was taken into consideration, combined with the effects of coaching and the implementation of profit sharing, everyone began to realize that there was a lot more room for growth in the market.

"We've established goals for the business group across the board now," says Liu. "The challenge this year is to achieve 50% growth, and looking at the most recent monthly numbers we can pull this off. We've already met the quotas for the first quarter. This year's goal is to make ourselves the world's third leading components maker. And by 2010, we plan to open seven new factories. We want to make Dongguan a bigger center for electronics components, but we also want our colleagues to open factories in their home provinces, so that workers don't need to leave home. The first has already opened in Hunnan province, and another will open next year in Jiangxi province."

Liu hasn't stopped learning. He made an appearance as an assistant coach at a recent Coaching program in Shenzhen and spoke about how coaching was spreading to Taiwan. Later, when asked how he finds the time to join coaching courses as an assistant, he said he takes time out because he finds it valuable to spend time with new-comers to a coaching environment, adding that he is still learning about himself.

"One important thing I learned from coaching," says Liu, "is that it's not about what you say, but about what you do. What you do counts for everything." 人

# Chapter 10

# From
# **RAGS** to
# **RICHES**

Z hou Xiaoguang, the 43-year-old president of the
Neoglory Group and representative to China's National
People's Congress, is the city of Yiwu's "iron lady." A
famously determined woman, she has built from nothing a
massive jewelry business with more than 5,600 employees and
assets worth more than 200 million yuan (US$24 million). Zhou's
life has been a uniquely Chinese rags-to-riches story, a personal
example of the remarkable transition that has shaken China in its
transition to a market economy.

Zhou was born in Zhuji, a mountainous area not far from Yiwu, a city of around one million in the central coastal province of Zhejiang, around four hours' drive south of Shanghai. Today, Yiwu is one of China's busiest wholesale markets, a major exporting center for small commodities such as clothing accessories – zippers and the like – and ornaments, and the city center is scattered with halal restaurants, catering to the large numbers of Middle Eastern businessmen who shop there. But during Zhou's childhood, Yiwu was just another nondescript middle-tier Chinese city that offered nothing in the way of opportunities for anyone who wasn't employed by a state-owned enterprise.

The eldest of seven children – six girls and one boy – Zhou grew up in an extended family that also included her father's parents. Like so many mountain villages in China in the 1960s, her home-town was so poor it had no road connecting it with the outside world.

"My childhood influenced me in three ways," she says. "First, I learned responsibility at an early age. Because I was the eldest daughter, I had to look after the little ones. When times were hard – and they were hard most of the time – I had to help my parents with whatever work was available, so I never had the experience of playing after school. There were always chores to do – cutting grass, chopping up wood, carrying the young ones around. There was never a moment's peace. But the second thing I got from my childhood was love and affection. We were very poor, but my family never fought – even when we didn't have enough to eat, or enough warm clothes to go around. In our village there were many families who shouted at and fought with one another, but we never did. We were a loving family, and very giving – always ready to help others, even when we weren't really in a position to do so. And that's the third thing my childhood gave me – a sense of the importance of giving. You did what you could to help other people. If you saw an old man struggling as he carried something, you would go over and help him. It was the normal thing to do – to help people without thinking about whether you were going to get anything in return."

But if it was a childhood that taught Zhou virtues, the poverty was grinding. "Every year when Chinese New Year came around, at the end of a long winter, and with spring still some time off in the mountains, there were shortages of food and warm clothes. It was a regular occurrence. My mother used to cook big pots of rice soup. It was funny stuff. When you ate it you'd feel full, but then 10 minutes later you'd be starving again. My parents, I still remember, were as skinny as scarecrows. And those pots of rice soup, with some green vegetables thrown in, that my mother cooked every day are my most vivid memory. The kids would wolf it all down, leaving only the soup stock for my parents to eat. As soon as I was old enough to realize what was happening, I tried to eat as little of the rice and vegetables as I could myself, but it was hard to do as a growing child.

The selflessness of my parents, and the sacrifices they made for their children, made an impression on me that will stay with me the rest of my life."

 ## ON THE ROAD

When Zhou was 17, she and her mother started to do a little business to try and bring in some extra cash for the family. They began making embroidered pillowslips at home, and then setting off on road trips across China to sell them.

"The traveling was very tough. In the winter we'd head south, and when summer was approaching we went north. To get to the northeast, it took four days and three nights – one night to get to Shanghai, where you changed trains, and another two nights to Harbin. Often there were no seats, so by day we would stand and at night we slept under the seats. From 1978 to 1986, eight years altogether, I traveled across half of China, through every kind of weather you can imagine – from snow and sleet to incredible heat and typhoon rains."

Zhou and her mother had to stay on the move partly because in those days private enterprise was frowned upon, but there were other factors also. "You couldn't stay in one place for too long because people would start to notice you and they would think it strange that women so far from home were on the street selling things. Even if we found a good spot, the longest we would stay in one place was two or three days because we were only selling one kind of product and there was a limited number of customers for our embroidery. We would go to wherever there was a department store, wherever there were passers-by, and lay out a mat. We looked for places that women went shopping, but we were often chased away when employees in the department store or in nearby shops noticed us. It was exhausting not being able to have a permanent place to sell things. It was like being a refugee. We scrimped and saved as much as we could. We ate as little as possible, and slept in the cheapest hostels – one yuan a night – so that we could save as much money as we could to take home with us.

"For years we stood on trains with our luggage containing more than 50 kilograms of embroidery – two huge boxes. There was no freight carriage in those days, so we had to carry everything ourselves. We had no way of knowing how many months it would take to sell everything and there were no telephones then, so you couldn't ring home. There was no popping home for a quick visit either, because it was too expensive. I often tell the story nowadays of how I wandered around China with all that embroidery, and stood in railway stations waiting for trains, crying and wondering how long I would have to live that kind of life. The only happy times were when we made it home and we had two or three hundred yuan in savings."

By the time she married in 1985, Zhou knew that it was a life that had to end, though she still did one more trip with a newly born son. But in April 1986, en route once again for the northeast with her infant son in tow, she realized she couldn't go on. "It was evening, and pouring with rain, and my husband accompanied us to the train station. I was standing on the platform, and when it came time to board the train, I knew all of a sudden that I wasn't going. I said to my husband, 'I don't want to go.' Without saying a word, he took the bags and got on the train, and I stayed behind. It was a turning point. If I'd gone that night, I'm not sure if I would have started my small jewelry business in Yiwu. Everything we did from 1986 to 1995 started from that moment."

While her husband was on the road in 1986, Zhou began to teach herself to make jewelry. She made excursions to Shanghai and Guangzhou to buy supplies, and she and one of her sisters worked late into the evenings making simple rings and brooches for sale in the Yiwu market. As the business grew, she brought in a few friends to help out in the evenings. In the beginning, her goal was to save enough money to buy a house and some furniture, and within a year she had saved 10,000 yuan (US$1,250). By 1995, Zhou and her husband had a house and several hundred thousand yuan in savings.

"We had gained a lot of experience and a lot of friends by that time," she says. "My experience of traveling all around China meant that I had a good understanding of the cultures and backgrounds of people from all over the country, and more and more of them were coming to Yiwu to buy our jewelry. The business was going so well by 1995 that we decided to open a factory. It was the beginning of Neoglory and a new chapter in my life."

## A CHANCE ENCOUNTER

By 1997, with the business growing faster than she had ever imagined, Zhou was playing catch-up with her education, snatching time for courses in Beijing, Shanghai, Hangzhou, and Shenzhen. She and her network of business associates and friends shared information with each other about useful courses they had attended. In 2001, while attending a course in Shanghai, a friend of Zhou's called Chen Yong told Zhou that a course was coming up in November that he had heard a lot about recently. "I told him to fax the information over to me, and after taking one look I decided to enroll. In the end, 11 of us went on the *Ren* Coaching program. We had no idea what it was we were going to learn, but I had a feeling from the publicity material I'd seen that it would be something useful. All 11 of us got through the first course, and then we all signed up for the other courses. No one dropped out. By the time I'd completed all the courses, I had encouraged more than 100 other people to enroll."

Unlike many people who first encounter coaching, Zhou had no resistance to this new experience. "I'd been attending courses for years by this point, and I was open to everything. I could see what coaching was basically about from the beginning, and I could also see that it was going to be very useful for me. I hadn't had much of an education, so I always took the position that anyone had the potential to be my teacher. For me, running a business, the one thing I knew was that I needed to keep improving. If I didn't improve, the business couldn't improve. I was very clear about that. Essentially, I was the force behind the development of the business, but equally I could be the force that held it back. I knew that I needed more than willpower to succeed. Knowledge and skills were equally important, and the only way I was going to get them was through study."

For Zhou, coaching brought immediate changes – changes that were obvious to her colleagues and friends. "It changed the way I looked at people and myself," says Zhou. "But I was also looking at problems differently, too. I started to look at things more objectively. I was learning to distance myself from my emotions. Without realizing it, we often have prejudices toward people we're dealing with, but when we do that we're being emotional. Coaching taught me to see that in myself, and to approach people with more tolerance and understanding. All of us have different standards, but too often we're only focused on our own standards. We impose our standards on our employees without thinking about what *their* standards might be. We might be frustrated by one of our managers, when the real problem is that he or she is unable to reach the standards we have imposed. From a coaching perspective, this is when we need to make an adjustment. After all, adaptation is something we're all good at. We just need to put time and planning into helping the person grow. Rather than criticizing them or dressing them down for their bad performance, we can help them to adjust."

Zhou began to look at human resources very differently after experiencing coaching. "I started to look at people and think, is this a skills problem or is it something about the person? Problems related to a person's skills and problems related to personality or attitude are things that can easily be distinguished. Sometimes an employee lacks specific skills that are needed to coordinate with a team in a work environment, and at other times it is a personality or attitude problem that is affecting their ability to coordinate with the group and put their skills into practice. From a coaching perspective, these are things we can help them differentiate between and overcome."

## TAKING ON THE CHALLENGE

After taking the course, Zhou had a revelation that changed her outlook on her life. "I found myself looking back and summing up my life and work, everything I'd been through. I had the sense of a real breakthrough. It was as if I was suddenly able to let go of a lot of old grievances I'd nurtured for far too long, and that made me feel like there was nothing I couldn't let go of. This baggage I'd been dragging around with me was suddenly gone, and I felt like I could face life and work in a much more relaxed kind of way. One important thing I realized was that for a long time I'd felt like I'd spent my entire life giving, but I'd never really thought about the fact that people around me were aware of it and appreciated it. When we played one of the games I chose to give up, but most people wanted me to take my place to be the team leader. It got me thinking about the fact that I had more support around me than I had realized before, and that made me feel like I could take on even more than I had in the past."

It was a pivotal moment for Zhou, and it led her to make a decision to put herself forward as Yiwu's representative for China's National People's Congress (NPC) in 2002. "It was not something I'd thought about doing before, but once the idea came to me and I started ringing around and saying to people that I wanted to run, it was as if the whole city came to my support. But it was an exhausting process, campaigning for the position, and without the support and encouragement I got through coaching I don't think I could have done it."

In 2005, Zhou earned the nickname "Queen of the NPC" for her reputation for putting forward more draft motions in the Congress than any other representative. Conducting an investigation into China's more than 90,000 wholesale markets – which are now thought to account for around a third of China's retail sales – Zhou found them lacking both government supervision and legal safeguards. She has also petitioned on land conservation issues and better handling of cross-provincial crimes, as well as sponsoring local TV advertisements to solicit public opinions on other issues that could be raised at the NPC. "I felt like I should make the most out of my five-year term, and not let the people of Yiwu down. The last thing I wanted was people saying, 'We shouldn't have voted for her.' It's an attitude I owe to coaching."

 ## BRINGING IT HOME

Zhou has taken her time bringing a coaching culture into the sprawling Neoglory Group. Initially, she simply encouraged her immediate family and most senior management personnel to undergo the *Ren* Coaching program, but in mid-2006 she launched a program to institute coaching principles at all management levels.

"Coaching can make an enormous difference in the private sector," she says. "The problem for so many of China's SMEs is that they were founded by people who not that long ago were working in the fields and who started out doing a bit of business on the side. People like us got the opportunities we have because of the introduction of a market economy, but because that has happened so suddenly a lot of us don't have the skills and knowledge we need to take advantage of the opportunities as effectively as we could. And attitude is another problem – it's something that many entrepreneurs have never really thought about in the way that coaching forces you to. Attitude is about who you are doing this for, and what exactly it is that you are doing. Many people don't understand this, and they are constantly looking for things to blame – complaining about business, about society, about this person and that person, about family, and so on. And as I see it, when those complaints start, it's a sure sign that the business is on the way to becoming unhealthy."

Zhou is in regular contact with entrepreneurs at all levels, but feels that too few of them have insight into themselves. "They feel they're overworked and exhausted, but the real problem is they don't have any objectivity about themselves and their working situations. For me, this was where coaching helped. Another common problem in the private sector is constant conflicts between entrepreneurs and their employees – usually, conflicts over how to distribute interests – and again, this is usually an attitude problem. They're thinking they're the boss, not an entrepreneur. Actually, being a boss and being an entrepreneur are intrinsically different things. When you're a boss, you're controlling other people — repressing them, even. But when you're an entrepreneur, you're creating a culture in which employees are happy to work among other employees, integrating everyone into a shared culture, a culture that has been made through teamwork, not one that has been created by control. Essentially, it's about equality. Equality means you respect me, I respect you; not 'I'm going to use my authority, my power, to control you.'"

Too many local small and medium-size enterprises, according to Zhou, have no human resources management, and in most cases there isn't even an awareness of what human resources are. Bosses rule from on high, and there is no teamwork aimed at meeting collective goals. "Being at the helm of a growing enterprise means involving people, bringing them in and advancing collective goals, not simply meeting your own goals. This is where a lot of entrepreneurs go wrong. They don't know how to employ human resources. For me, the breakthrough came when I encountered coaching. In my experience, this is basic: we have to respect each other, understand each other, tolerate each other. Too many entrepreneurs are full of themselves and can only see things from their own perspectives. They have no respect for alternative opinions and simply don't listen when someone is expressing a point of view that differs from their own. And that's where coaching can make all the difference."

Respecting and listening to alternative points of view doesn't mean forgetting your own, says Zhou. Coaching, after all, is largely about helping clients to have clarity about their own direction, their own goals. "When I'm talking to someone now, I'm thinking about what exactly it is I want to say. What result do I want to achieve? My thinking has a definite direction. In the past, that wasn't the case. But now I know what I'm talking about when I'm talking with people – I know where I'm taking things. I'm clear in my mind, and that's been a big help to me.

"Of course, we all have more than one goal in life. I have life goals, goals for my family, career goals, but my overall goal is for Neoglory. We're now the biggest jewelry business in China. The goal now is to become an internationally recognized brand name. That's a company goal. We want to win some glory for China, and make Neoglory an influential brand name."

PART 3

# THE *TAO* OF **REN:**
## NINE-DOT
## LEADERSHIP

Chapter **11**

# Making
# **DREAMS** a
# **REALITY**

**T**wo cornerstones of a Confucian education were the classic texts *The Great Learning* and *The Doctrine of the Mean*. The first features a short introduction by Confucius himself, followed by a longer analysis by one of his disciples, while *The Doctrine of the Mean* is said to have been written by Confucius's grandson. Neither book is particularly long, but both have been enormously influential in Chinese politics and society for more than 20 centuries. What is the message that has guaranteed these books such an enormously long shelf-life? In the case of *The Great Learning*, it is that ordering the state begins with the improvement of the individual. Confucius's message concludes with the words: "From the Son of Heaven down to the people, all must consider the cultivation of the person the root of everything else." *The Doctrine of the Mean*, on the other hand, concentrates on the harmony that must exist between one's inner self and one's surroundings: "Only when a man lives in accordance with his knowledge of both nature and people, and becomes a well-learned person, can he manage his country and the world."

Many modern Chinese, not to mention non-Chinese, who today read these texts find them a little difficult to understand with their archaic language and sometimes obscure references. But their essential message is actually very simple: observe your outside environment, know yourself – and harmonize the two. Of course, knowing your inner self and harmonizing it with your environment is easier said than done. We must wonder what proportion of the many millions of scholars who have committed Confucius's text to memory in preparation for imperial exams over the centuries actually put his words into practice. But then, what does harmonizing our inner and outer lives really have to do with the real issues we have to face in life, such as maintaining a relationship, running the accounts of a marketing department, or motivating our staff to turn up at that important meeting on Monday morning?

When we turn to these practical questions with our clients in China, we start with the character *ren*. After all, the Confucian classics may be inspiring, gorgeously crafted works, but at the end of the day, they are somewhat lecturing in tone, and most of us have a tendency to switch off when we are being told what to do – no matter how good the advice may be. Far better that we find our own advice. But, for most of us, that requires something of an awakening. By returning to that simple Chinese character and analyzing its components and hidden potentialities, we begin the journey to an awakening of what it means to be human.

So, let us look again at *ren*: two broad brush-strokes; one flowing down, the other swinging up. Perfectly balanced and in total harmony. Without one, the other would surely totter and fall. But wait, *ren* is equally clearly defined by its extremities: its three terminal points – or perhaps that should be beginnings – of the strokes that comprise its structure.

We call these elements of the *ren* character the Two Aspects and the Three Pillars.

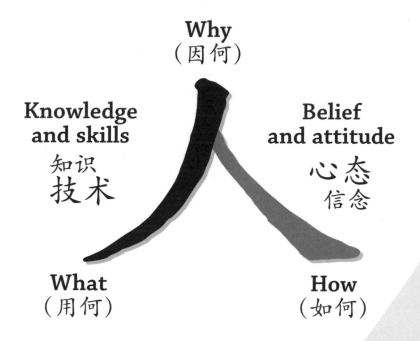

## TWO ASPECTS

We have made many references to our inner and outer selves, to the inner and outer games. But what exactly are these two aspects of our lives?

Everyone has an inner self and an outer self. The inner is hidden, rarely coming into play in ways that we ourselves recognize. But at the same time it exerts an enormous influence on our behavior and on the directions we take in our lives. In this sense, the inner self is rather similar to Freud's concept of the subconscious. While for Freud, however, the subconscious was a dark place that needed to be liberated and illuminated by psychoanalysis, the *Ren* Coaching Model treats the inner self as something people can be awakened into recognizing and developing.

The outer self is what we consciously express to the world, or what we have consciously acquired through study – the professional skills and qualifications, say, that we have amassed over the years in a career. Thus, you might say that our inner selves are our hidden potential, while our outer selves are our knowledge and skills.

Laozi, the great Taoist sage, once said: "In pursuit of knowledge, we gain day by day." But then he added: "In the pursuit of the way (*dao*), we discard day by day." A typically Taoist conundrum, Laozi is not being as obscure as he seems at first glance. He is saying that in order to improve, we need both to learn – and to unlearn. Think of the things that have to be discarded as certain old ideas, certain tired behavior ticks, certain conventions. We cast away these things to gain new possibilities, which is a way of throwing off the past in order to gain the future. Another way of putting this is that the knowledge we learn day by day may improve our outer selves, while the things we discard day by day improve our inner selves.

Embracing both of these processes – simultaneously gaining and losing – is the essence of the *Ren* Coaching Model, and it brings us back to our lesson about the *ren* character and the twirling man who symbolizes "reform." Without reform, there is no hope of improving either by consciously gaining knowledge or by discarding unconsciously self-imposed boundaries.

To put this in more practical terms, so much of what we learn in life is for the development of our careers – or so we think. When we pass through the education system, we study subjects such as literature, mathematics, and physics. We learn professional skills such as marketing and finance. And in the process of acquiring these skills, we take pride in the way we are improving every day by enhancing our knowledge. But how often do we stop to look at this vast accumulation of baggage and ask ourselves whether it is time for a spring clean? Or the even more probing question: Is this untidy accumulation of things I've picked up along the way the sum of me?

This questioning from the inner self and directed at the outer self is an ongoing act of reformation with the ultimate aim of harmonizing the two aspects of the self. Without it, the outer self is likely to become bowed down with the weight of all it has to lug on its journey, and fail to put it to good use. This has long been recognized in the Chinese tradition, as we have already seen. The sages of old would have recognized, for instance, that there is no difference between skills and knowledge obtained by training in martial arts or in a modern MBA degree if the inner self is not simultaneously questioning and growing with the skills the outer self is acquiring. An MBA graduate has a certificate and a new set of skills, but if his inner self has no sense of what he needs from this knowledge, all he has is window dressing. The martial artist may learn, say, to wield a sword, but until he is at one with the sword he is simply two imperfectly matched objects – a man and a sword.

The man who is at one with his sword doesn't need to brandish it. He is like the sales and marketing professional who doesn't need to brag about his product in order to make a sale. He has transcended the product, so that his own personal qualities speak for it as much as the product itself.

Confucius and Laozi realized this more than two millennia ago. Today, the *Ren* Coaching Model is showing Chinese executives and their staff that this wisdom is just as applicable in the modern workplace as it has been throughout the ages in traditional Chinese society.

## THREE PILLARS

If *ren* has two aspects, it also has three supporting pillars. They are rather like a code for a safe – only when all three are in complete alignment can the door to the safe be opened. Crowning them is the word *Yin*, which is from the Chinese Buddhist term for "cause and effect," but which here is best translated as *Why*. Think of this as a querying of the fundamentals, rather than literally questions prefaced by the word "why" – as in, "Why haven't I won the lottery yet and retired to the south of France?" *Why* in this case encompasses questions such as: "Why *do I want* to win the lottery and retire to the south of France?" or "*Why* do I want to retire?" It symbolizes a life led with an open-minded and healthily questioning outlook, unlike that led by the person who has already made up his mind about everything.

Turning to the right pillar, we see the word *Tao*, the Confucian and Taoist term for "the way"; here, more simply, it means *How*. What springs to mind when we see this is the notion, "*How* do I get to where I'm going?" But actually the question is inner-directed rather than outer-directed. If *Yin*, or *Why*, sets us to asking questions about our motives, then *Tao*, or *How*, asks us how we can be ourselves. In a sense, it is the crucial harmonizing question at the heart of the *Ren* Coaching Model. If we adopt an open-minded spirit of questioning, every question we ask is about how we can best be ourselves.

That leaves us with the left pillar, *Shu*, which is from the Chinese word *jishu*, meaning "skills", but which here means *What*. *Shu*, in other words, is the practical element of the equation – the *What*, or the skills and tools, we need to move forward with our harmonized outer- and inner-directed selves. In other words, what do we need in order to get to where it is we know, deep in our hearts, that we want to go? In ancient oracle script, the character for skill (术 – *shu*) actually means "path" or "road." According to Zhang Yi's *Guangya Shigu*, a dictionary of ancient Chinese characters, skills are the path and method that take us to our goal, or destination.

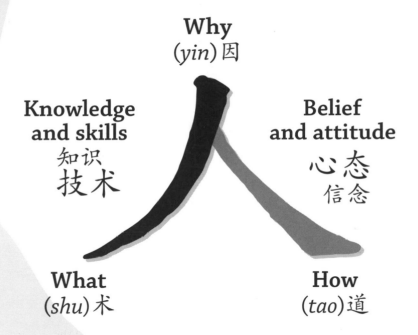

**Why**
(*yin*) 因

**Knowledge and skills**
知识
技术

**Belief and attitude**
心态
信念

**What**
(*shu*) 术

**How**
(*tao*) 道

An inspiring example of a successful person who has harmonized the *Yin*, *Tao*, and *Shu* of his life is Howard Schultz, the founder of Starbucks. The original store opened in Seattle, in the United States, in 1971; it was a small place that sold coffee beans and coffee accessories. Schultz, a coffee machine salesman, fell in love with the store the moment he first saw it in 1982. He quit his job and went to work at the store. Schultz's vision was that there was a huge potential market for gourmet coffee to be sold to on-the-go Americans, but it wasn't a vision that was shared by the original Starbucks' owners, and in 1985 Schultz established the Il Giornale coffee bar chain. In 1987, however, Schultz got the opportunity he had been waiting for, and was able to raise the money to buy out the now six branches of Starbucks in Seattle. He then re-branded his Il Giornale chain. By 1992, when Starbucks made its initial public offering, it had 165 outlets, but this was just the beginning of a massive phase of expansion that has taken the chain to 37 countries with some 11,000 outlets – and five new ones opening every day.

For Howard Schultz, Starbucks was about far more than selling coffee. A saying that was coined in the company's early days went: "We're not in the business of filling bellies; we're in the business of filling souls." Schultz saw Starbucks as bringing coffee to America through creating a warm environment, with jazz playing in the background and with lounging furniture; a halfway house between home and work. In short, Starbucks wasn't just bringing coffee to America, but coffee culture. Schultz's vision was the *Yin*, or *Why*, of his mission, while the culture that is embodied in every store is the *Tao*, or *How*. And the fact that these two qualities were so harmonized in Schultz made it possible for him to overcome all obstacles and mobilize the *Shu*, or *What*, so as to make it happen. In 1987 when Schultz was shopping around for investors for a chain of coffee stores selling coffee with strange Italian-sounding names at US$3 a cup, most people were skeptical on hearing his pitch. But Schultz's Three Pillars were perfectly harmonized and failure wasn't an option.

The *Ren* Coaching Model provides a way for anyone to achieve their potential. It blends Western and Chinese concepts and adapts them to a Chinese environment, reapplying ancient wisdom to daily life. Of course, we don't all want to run a global chain of coffee stores, but we can all lead fuller, more effective lives by becoming more aware of our true interests and goals, and of the inner obstacles that are standing in the way of our achieving them. Once the Three Pillars are clear to us and harmonized, everything becomes possible.

## A PLAN IN LIFE

The road we have traveled on to wherever we are now may have vanished behind us, but it is still beneath our feet, extending into the future. If we know where we are going, that road is clear. Some of us, however, don't even know where we stand now, let alone where the road is leading. But the present and the way ahead are actually all embodied in the *ren* character. *Yin*, or *Why*, enables us to understand the meaning of our path and its future direction; while *Tao*, or *How*, brings together our beliefs and attitudes; and *Shu*, or *What*, is the skills we need to bring into play if we want to start on the road to our destination and one day reach it.

Life is simply a series of experiences, and these experiences form our mindsets. These mindsets can block us, but why is that? The key is whether we understand ourselves or not. Do we know what we really want? Do we know what we desire? Do we understand where our attitudes originated and how they developed, and are they in line with each other or do they contradict? What is more, we can ask ourselves whether our skills are in line with what we are seeking. We can truly understand ourselves only by answering these questions; failure to do so produces a lack of self-awareness.

Self-awareness comes from understanding the Two Aspects – our inner and outer selves – and the Three Pillars of life. But the crucial element is *Yin*, or *Why*, and for a coach working with a client it is essential to illuminate this. After all, *Yin*, or *Why*, is the foundation of human existence, the mobilizing force for both our *Tao* and our *Shu*.

Put simply, *Yin* is essential to having a life plan because it sets a clear direction, establishing a vision, values, and goals that, in turn, lead to results. A life plan provides a client with a clear direction and objective in life. And this is where the coach comes in. Even if the client's contact with a coach is brief, the impact can be life-transforming in as much as it provides an opportunity to make a life plan.

A strong sense of direction is equal to having vision. In his book *The Fifth Discipline: The Art and Practice of the Learning Organization*, Peter Senge calls vision the force that makes people feel they have a deep calling. In the beginning it might be little more than a thought, but if it develops through nurture and support it ceases to be something abstract, and takes on an almost concrete existence. This is what authors Thomas J. Peters and Robert H. Waterman, Jr. refer to when they call vision "a journey from the known to the unknown," in their book *In Search of Excellence*. By this they mean that the future can be brought into being by combining present realities, hopes, dreams, and opportunities. Of course, having vision doesn't make it possible for us to predict the future, but it does provide us with a map to take us there.

As children we generally don't have a grand vision of our lives. It is only with experience that we find the real desires of our hearts and discover what we really want. Over time, vision can gradually manifest itself and become a powerful force to drive us toward our heart's desires. It is almost like a powerful magnetic field, and it is impossible to resist its gravitational pull. And the more clarity we have about our sense of vision, the stronger that pull will be.

Equally important to having a life plan, however, are values. But what, exactly, are values? Philosophers have debated their meaning for centuries. Perhaps, as some argue, there are no ultimate values, no intrinsic right and wrong. Nevertheless, the coach is still concerned about the values and motivations that drive the client, and how those values and motivations influence that person's life path and future. The task of the coach is to show the client, as objectively as possible, the correlation between their values and the path they have chosen to take, while at the same time not being a judge of right and wrong. Only the client can be the judge of that.

If we think of life as being like a jigsaw puzzle, our vision is the picture that is waiting to be completed. We put the puzzle together one piece at a time. With each year of our life, we add another piece to our puzzle, and choosing the right piece at any time depends on what stage of life we are at. We need to think about how it will interconnect with the other pieces we have already put in place. In other words, we need to set very clear goals and be able to come up with steps to achieve them.

When a client's goal is something they really want, they will have a strong desire to overcome any difficulties that stand in their path, but a coach should not be satisfied with this alone. The coach has to address the *Yin*, or *Why*. What is driving a client to attain their goal? In this way, the coach combines the goal, the vision, and the values, resulting in a more clearly defined goal. Between a goal and results lies an important link: action. Action isn't just a way of turning goals into results; it is also a way of transforming our vision into a tangible reality. Action planning, in other words, is another crucial step in the coaching process.

**Goal**
目标

**Result**
成果

**Action**
行动

Vision and values are like an internal map. Vision may tell us where we are going, but values tell us why. Meanwhile, action is the link between goals and results, the *Shu* of our journey.

## THE ADAPTIVE CHALLENGE

Coaching returns us to the basics in our lives – our reasons for doing things and our purpose – and in this sense it is a form of leadership. But to really understand the connection between leadership and coaching, we need to look at the concept of adaptive leadership. Consider the case of a patient visiting his doctor. Generally, this will involve three different scenarios.

In the first, and most frequent, situation the patient describes his symptoms, and the doctor provides a prescription and instructions for restoring good health. The patient trusts the doctor, and the doctor is confident about his diagnosis and suggested treatment. Relying on the professional knowledge of the doctor, the patient transfers responsibility for his health to the doctor.

In the second scenario, the doctor identifies the problem but has no clear way to cure the root cause of the illness. An example might be a diagnosis of heart disease. The doctor can provide instructions that will likely lead to better health, but he cannot guarantee they will lead to complete recovery. For example, the doctor will likely caution the patient about diet and exercise, and tell him to avoid stress. In this sense, the doctor may well have the key to curing the patient's illness, but he is not responsible for it – only the patient can be. It is a situation, in other words, in which both the doctor and the patient are responsible for the problem's solution.

In the third scenario, the doctor is confronted with an illness he has never come across before and the cause of which is obscure. It is a situation in which the doctor's past experience is of no great use to him. The result is that the doctor and the patient carry out in-depth discussions and identify possible problems and their causes. The discussions are frank, and the doctor and the patient work together to come up with a course of treatment.

At the heart of each of these scenarios is the issue of technicalities, as opposed to the challenge of being adaptive. Introduced by Ronald A. Heifetz, co-founder of the Center for Public Leadership at the John F. Kennedy School of Government, Harvard University, adaptive leadership assumes that, broadly speaking, leaders face two scenarios: technical problems and adaptive challenges. In the case of a technicality, the problem and its solution are clear, and the job of a leader is to provide that solution to those with less experience or knowledge. In the case of a problem that requires adaptation, however, there is no obvious solution, and it is necessary to adapt to it cooperatively. For Heifetz, leadership is an *activity*, and that activity is mobilizing adaptive change.

Heifetz, a doctor of psychiatry, arrived at the distinction between technicalities and adaptation through working with his patients. But the implications of adaptive leadership extend far beyond psychiatry; they reach out to society as a whole, including businesses. In general, after all, leadership tends to be focused on technicalities. Leadership is entrusted to people who take responsibility and have an ability to solve problems. In a traditional system, leadership is an authority, rarely seeking alternative views from subordinates. In turn, employees tend to become followers, having very little independence of thought.

In a stable business environment marked by little competition, this is a leadership model that can work. But in a business environment marked by intense competition and rapidly changing market conditions, the ability to adapt becomes a necessity. Reliance on old patterns of authority in such circumstances can actually get in the way of adaptation, due to a vicious circle that negatively impacts on both the leader and those being led. People who are used to following orders will turn to authority for their next move because that is what they have become accustomed to in the past, and so the group comes increasingly to depend on the decision-making of its leadership. The more the group submits itself, the more it becomes helpless and unwilling to take responsibility. Meanwhile, the leader, responding to these expectations, becomes accustomed to exercising power, and will start to feel the need to protect it. This is particularly the case when decisions handed down from on high fail to resolve problems. The authority of the leader will start to be questioned within the group, leading to conflict and a lack of cohesion. On the one hand, the group will look to authority for leadership, and on the other doubt its powers to resolve problems. Once enough resistance accumulates, indifference will begin to take over. Superficially, staff will appear to be committed to the leader, but in reality work is not getting done.

Adaptive leadership, however, deals with problems in an altogether different way. It may very well identify the problem but it is just one of the agents in finding a solution. This is a situation in which authority is dispersed. The main responsibility of the leader is to help the group face conflicts that have arisen from their differing values, to understand what is involved in various courses of action, and to learn to adapt and revise their belief systems, actions, and values. The next step is to respond to the external environment experimentally, but with a plan of action. In an adaptive environment like this, employees are the main assets of the company, and the leader is just their legally empowered agent.

Modern human resources emphasizes the importance of effecting a transition from "*You* want me to do it" to "*I* want to do it." This is a transition from the passive to the active, allowing people to take responsibility for themselves. It is not a change that a technical approach can achieve. Only an adaptive approach can make the change.

## 🔳 THE *TAO* OF COACHING

Confronting change is difficult, and more often than not we try to deal with it either through technical means or through a strategy of evasion. But both approaches are flawed: the technical approach will often fail to solve the problem at its root, while evasion simply involves shifting responsibility from one person to another person. This is why adaptive strategies have to be adopted early when facing change. Change can be seen as threatening and may make people feel uneasy. But by being adaptive, people are able to face threats head on, accommodate themselves to their changing environment, find new roles for themselves, and tap into their creativity in finding solutions. With time, being adaptive becomes a naturally ongoing process.

But what precisely is leadership that embraces the adaptive challenge doing? First and foremost, it is shifting beliefs and attitudes, and it can only be effective when everyone involved is *willing* to shift their beliefs and attitudes. The first requirement for that to happen is an equivalent commitment from the leadership. Until leadership is aware of the benefits for staff of shifting from "*You* want me to do it" to "*I* want to do it," nothing will change. The second requirement, of course, is that the group itself has to be willing to embrace the concept of "*I* want to do it."

This is where coaching comes in. It challenges previously rigid behaviors and opens up belief systems, helping people to react positively to changing environments, and converting uneasiness into creativity. Generally, adaptive leadership and coaching are seen as separate studies and practices, but at their heart they are both about the same thing: adaptation. The coach adapts the beliefs and attitudes of the client through dialog, empowering the client to find his own answers, establish a plan of action, and achieve targets. The relationship between the coach and the client is one of mutual trust, and their common objective is to achieve the client's goals. And in this sense a coach is different from other professionals such as consultants, psychologists, and trainers. Even though coaches, in the scope of their professional field, are authorities, in the practice of coaching they don't act as an authority. The coach and the client are equals, exploring and learning together. Coaching isn't about giving orders, controlling, or supervising, but is a process of deep exploration.

Consultants tend to focus on issues, not on people. A consultant uses information and data to provide professional suggestions and solutions to his clients – unlike a coach, who doesn't provide answers. Counselors and psychiatrists focus on the past, working to resolve old issues and psychological imbalances, whereas a coach focuses on the future, goal-setting, and action. Coaching differs from training also. A trainer provides knowledge and skills to athletes, while a coach helps the client to discover their strengths, identify blind spots, and explore their innate abilities in order to achieve results.

The adaptive challenge is all around us, and adaptive leadership has value to everyone. Put simply, leadership is the ability to achieve higher goals together with other people. The *Ren* Coaching Model emphasizes leadership because each and every one of us lives in a group, interacting with the outside world, cooperating with others to achieve our goals. Leadership ability is hidden within each one of us. The *Ren* Coaching Model is a method for tapping into that potential and exploring it to the full.

 ## THE NINE-DOT GAME

Beliefs and attitudes are at the heart of leadership, as we have seen, and through years of experience we have identified nine core beliefs and attitudes that are essential to effective leadership. We call this the Nine-Dot Leadership Model, but before we describe it let us play the nine-dot game. Below are nine dots. How do you connect these nine dots using only four straight lines and without lifting your pen?

How did you do? It's not easy, is it? Most people who play this game for the first time find themselves stumped, and a common reaction, after many attempts, is to conclude that it cannot be done. This is rather similar to the way many people regard difficult situations in life. They approach problems based on previous experience and come to the conclusion that they cannot be solved. But to return to the game, is it really impossible? Try extending the straight lines outside the box and see what happens.

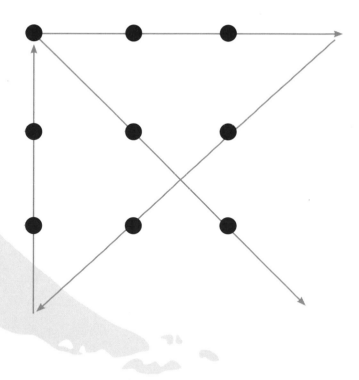

In fact, the answer was there all along. But for a coach, that isn't the important thing. What *is* important is what was preventing the client from finding the answer. If the client had obstacles that made it difficult to find the answer to the nine-dot game, what other answers are eluding the client in life and work?

## BETWEEN THE "FISH AND THE BEAR'S PAW"

Sometimes, it is necessary for a coach to challenge a client to adapt to a problem they think is insurmountable.

One client wanted to join a training program in Hong Kong, but then discovered at the last minute that it clashed with an important business conference in Vietnam. Suddenly, he was, as the Chinese saying goes, unable to decide between the "fish and the bear's paw" – two delicacies at a Chinese feast in times gone by, when eating bears was still socially acceptable.

The coach challenged him to do both.

It seemed impossible. There was no direct flight from Vietnam to Hong Kong, and the timing for both events was too close for comfort. Nevertheless, the businessman managed to finish his conference in Vietnam in time to catch a flight back to Hong Kong for the training, even though it involved two transit stops en route.

The coach had effectively challenged the businessman's notion that he was dealing with two conflicting events. This is worthwhile because often, when we view two things – say, having a career and having a family at the same time – as conflicting from the start, we find it harder to juggle them. But when we view them as complementary, then it is easier to find a solution.

But also we need to challenge ourselves to recognize whether we are confronted with something we are unwilling or unable to adapt to, because generally both amount to the same thing: "This is something I haven't dealt with before and it must be impossible."

When we challenge ourselves, we usually find we are far more adaptive than we imagined before.

##  THE NINE-DOT LEADERSHIP MODEL

In the Nine-Dot Leadership Model, the dots begin with passion. With passion comes commitment, and with commitment comes responsibility, and appreciation of everything around you. With appreciation comes giving, which inspires trust and generates win-win situations. A win-win situation fires passion and an enthusiasm for enrollment.

### 9-dot Leadership©
九点领导力©

In the diagram above, the ninth "dot" of leadership is a question mark. What is missing in the equation? Most people who try to work it out give up after a few attempts and admit they don't know. But for a coach, "I don't know" is the perfect answer. It provides food for thought. What is more, it provides infinite possibilities. And, in fact, "possibilities" is precisely the word that is needed to complete the Nine-Dot Leadership Model.

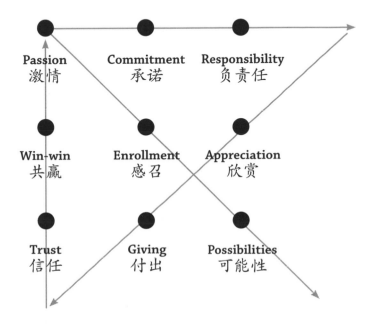

## 9-dot Leadership©
### 九点领导力©

The nine-dot game pushes people to think beyond the conventions they impose on themselves, while the Nine-Dot Leadership Model enables them to break free of those conventions, to banish their self-imposed limitations, strengthen their adaptive and creative leadership, and free them to explore life in all its complexity.

The Nine-Dot Leadership Model is like the hand of a compass; it can point to the blind spots in clients' hearts, and help them to find their true direction in life. This means looking into ourselves for the reasons things are as they are, rather than looking to externals. As Confucius put it: "In archery there is something of the man of virtue; if a man misses his target, he must look for the cause in himself." This is similar to the English expression that says, "A bad workman blames his tools." In all things in life, it is necessary to cast our heads back in our own direction. Only through knowing ourselves can we know others, and only through knowing others can we understand issues, further illuminating ourselves.

Passion, commitment, responsibility, appreciation, giving, trust, win-win, enrollment, and possibilities form the Nine-Dot Leadership Model. Superficially, such words are easy to understand, but they take on far deeper meanings when we strive to live by them. The essence of coaching is to strip away what experience has us believe we "know" about the meanings of these words. After all, our jobs and our social backgrounds influence how we see the world. For example, shown a child's drawing of a circle, a chef might say the circle is an egg, a physicist an atom, while a fashion model might think it is a mirror. The aim of coaching is to return us to things free of our social conditioning

– to see the circle drawn by a child as a circle drawn by a child. Our conditioning is essentially what we have learned. Most of us think of learning as what we have learned from books. But for a coach, learning from books is about externals – knowledge and skills that others have summarized – and has nothing to do with the real work that confronts us of looking within ourselves.

 ## 1. Passion

"Only those who are absolutely sincere can fully develop their nature. By fully developing their nature, they can fully develop the nature of others. By fully developing the nature of others, they can fully develop the nature of things. Those who fully develop the nature of things are worthy to assist in the transforming and nourishing process of heaven and earth. Those worthy to assist in the transforming and nourishing process of heaven and earth can thus form a trinity with heaven and earth." –*The Doctrine of the Mean*

In modern terms, this quote from one of the classic Confucian texts is saying that only when a person is honest and sincere can they fully manifest their true "I" or self. It is only in the expression of their real selves that they can realize the true nature of others, and in turn it is only then that they can realize the nature of things and align themselves with heaven and earth.

At the heart of this classical wisdom is the importance of complete honesty, which has a powerful influence on anyone who embraces it. Honesty with oneself is a key source of passion. The person who is honest with themselves and pursues the direction their heart sets is naturally a passionate person. Passion is a powerful force. We can feel it in the air. We can sense it through words and actions, and it can spread like wildfire, influencing everyone it touches. A passionless person is like a pebble that, when dropped into water, creates no ripples. Those who lack passion always retreat in the face of challenge.

But where do we find passion? The *Ren* Coaching Model teaches that the *Yin*, or *Why*, of passion is true values, its *Tao*, or *How*, is freedom of choice, and its *Shu*, or *What*, is self-expression. When all three of these are in alignment, we are passionate.

 ## True Values

Think of Indian history and many people think immediately of Mahatma Gandhi. Wherever he went, excited crowds would gather. Groups of disciples were willing to follow him. He fought for most of his life for the independence and liberation of his

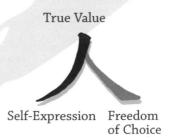

True Value

Self-Expression    Freedom of Choice

country. He also fought to eliminate the caste system and to remove conflict between Hindus and Muslims. He traveled around the country risking his life giving speeches. He often fasted. He was imprisoned many times, on the last occasion at the age of 73. In 1948, on his way to prayers, Gandhi was killed by a Hindu fanatic. But his spirit lives on and he is revered as a sacred hero.

Where did Gandhi find his energy, and his willingness to make the sacrifices he made? Unafraid of death, Gandhi was a living testament to the German philosopher Nietzsche's observation, "He who has *why* to live for can bear almost any *how*." In his determination against violence, his love of truth, his belief in living a simple life, and his hope to bring peace and self-determination to the people of India, Gandhi is one of the best models for understanding true self-value and the importance of the *Why* of living.

Understanding the *Why* of living brings us back to our true selves. As Laozi said, "*Tao* is learning from nature." We are all born in a state of nature, and our natural state is to state our wishes directly. Small children will cry out for a toy and sing without embarrassment in public. It is only as children grow up that their external environment teaches them conventional behavior patterns that limit their expression of their true selves. As time goes by, the true self can end up buried under the weight of conventions and values imposed by social conditioning. But when we allow imposed values to lead us, it is as if we are governed by external technical leadership, as opposed to adaptive internal leadership. Just as Gandhi did, we all need to acknowledge our true selves in order to embrace our true values. On a material level, Gandhi may have had nothing, but he lived a full life and inspired many millions of people to peaceful action.

When we allow artificial values to lead us, it is impossible to see what is important in life, and we can easily lose our sense of direction. We might think, for example, that we are unhappy because we don't have a Ferrari or a villa in Tuscany. These are artificial values, and while they can bring us temporary satisfaction they cannot satisfy the values that are innate in our hearts. We need to acknowledge our true selves in order to find our true values. This is precisely what Gandhi did. On the material level, he had nothing. Yet, he lived a full life and had an enormous influence on the world.

The 20th-century French philosopher Jean-Paul Sartre once wrote, "Man is nothing but what he makes of himself." This existentialist catch-cry was a way of saying that we are responsible for defining ourselves. But to define ourselves in keeping with our true selves, we need to be able to truthfully answer the questions, "What should I be?" or "What should I become?" And to be able to do this we need to be able to answer the question, "What are my true values?" To be able to do this, we all need to be able to establish what is innate in ourselves, to find the things that really stir our hearts. On the quest for passion, the coach's first step is to help the client find their true values.

 ## *Freedom of Choice*

During World War II, an Austrian Jew named Viktor Frankl was imprisoned and tortured for three years in a concentration camp. His parents, brother, and wife either died during their imprisonment or were sent to the gas chambers. Only Frankl and his younger sister survived. Frankl used willpower to beat the odds that were stacked against him, resuming his career as a neurologist and psychiatrist after the war, and writing *Man's Search for Meaning*, which sold more than five million copies in the United States alone.

Frankl's war experience was evidence for him that anything can be taken away from us except our freedom to choose. He realized that we have the freedom to adopt any attitude we like to the circumstances that befall us, and that this is our ultimate freedom. His personal observations showed him that the kind of prisoner a person becomes is actually a choice and is not dictated by their environment. A trying situation is an opportunity to nurture mental fortitude. In ordinary life, we have the same freedom to adopt an attitude, even though most of us choose not to take it. We act as if, under such and such circumstances, we have no choice but to be unhappy or frustrated or sad. But in doing so, we forget that we have the freedom to choose, and that means having the right to choose our own true values, and being able at any time to choose our attitudes and outlook on life.

Frankl's experience shows us that when we say things like, "The circumstances of my life are making me unhappy," or "It's all his or her fault," we are denying ourselves our right to freedom of choice. This is delusional behavior. Happiness and joy, and their opposites, are things we feel, and are not really related to what we do. We choose to be happy or unhappy, and that right to choose is entirely in our own hands. Similarly, we can choose to do something happily or unhappily.

## THE NEXT VILLAGE

"I've been held back by the town I grew up in," a client from the landlocked southern province of Hunan told his coach. "It's such a poor, backward place."

"So, are you suggesting that in your home-town there is no one who has prospered?" asked the coach.

"No," admitted the client.

"Well, if you share the same environment, why is it that some can do well and you cannot?"

In a flash, the client saw that he was confusing his environment with his destiny. It may be undeniable that our environment has an influence on us, but to depend on our environment for success is futile, and the biggest change we can make to our environment – as Frankl understood and taught – is to change ourselves.

A fable illustrates this point admirably. A traveler saw a village on the horizon and then noticed an old man sitting by the side of the road. "Is that village on the horizon a good place?" the traveler asked the old man.

"Which village did you come from?" the old man replied. "If your home village was a good place, then so is the village ahead of you. If your home-town was a bad place, then so is the place you are going to next."

In real life, "the next village" could be the next city, the next job, or the next marriage. Whether they are good is likely to be far more about us than it is about them.

This freedom of choice, though, shouldn't be confused with making the kinds of decisions we make on a daily basis, such as making an investment, buying a new toaster, or setting a goal for our business. Decisions like this are constrained by external factors. But we have complete freedom to determine our self-worth and our attitudes. When we choose what kind of person we want to be and become, external conditions cannot stop us from making that choice. This is what Frankl called "ultimate freedom," and as long as we have will, nothing can take this away from us.

Judging by material standards, the life that Gandhi chose was impoverished, as he had nothing to his name. Judging by his external conditions, Frankl's existence as a prisoner was miserable. But both these men found joy in the choices they made to embrace a positive attitude. They chose their own self-worth and lived fulfilling lives.

 *Self-expression*

Self-expression is about revealing the self without a mask, and being as sincere as possible. Take the conductor of an orchestra; his entire body, his facial expressions, are given over utterly to the music. In his immersion, he is totally immune to any sense that he might look foolish or invite criticism. Essentially, in other words, self-expression is a state of truth. But when does that happen? Only when we don't hide our feelings and express directly what is in our hearts. Small children laugh and cry without a thought, choosing freely and not disguising their feelings.

## THE REAL AND THE FAKE

A Chinese businessman who had been involved in international trade for many years remarked to one of our coaches that it disheartened him how so many people that he met lacked sincerity. He said that in the end he himself adopted a facade to deal with the phony and hypocritical people that came his way.

"So," said the coach, "you feel different from most of the other people you meet in business because there is something within yourself that is real. Isn't that rather like saying, 'There is at least one person who is real in this world, and that's myself'?"

"Yes, in a way I suppose I am saying something like that," said the businessman after a moment's thought.

"But how can there be something *real* unless there's something *fake*? Really, when we say that someone is being fake, we're expressing a sense that they're not being themselves."

"Yes," agreed the businessman with a slow smile. "When you put it like that, there's something real within everyone."

And, if you are willing to display *your* real self, there's an excellent chance that others will be willing to follow suit," concluded the businessman.

"We don't lack beauty in life," said the French sculptor Rodin. "What we lack is an eye for beauty."

The same goes for appreciation of those around us. Usually it takes some giving of ourselves for their true qualities to become apparent.

At the other extreme, take someone who habitually disguises their real feelings, as if they were a player in a stagy Cultural Revolution opera. Even if they say they are happy, it is very difficult to determine their real feelings. Like many of us, they have created a character for themselves in life, and the more others affirm this character the deeper it becomes ingrained in the person who has taken it on. Eventually, they are no longer living for themselves, and any expression of passion is impossible because their true self is buried.

The person with real passion embraces their sense of self-value, chooses their freedom to respond to any situation they find themselves in in a positive way, and is sincere in how they express themselves. This is the person of absolute sincerity who is the ideal of that Chinese classic, *The Doctrine of the Mean* – the person for whom heaven and earth are one.

##  2. Commitment

Many people think that they know how to commit, because they feel like they are always committing themselves. But take a look at the two Chinese characters that make up the word "commitment" (承) and (诺) The first character, pronounced *cheng*, means "to

bear" or "to carry." In "oracle bone" inscriptions of the character, its head resembles a person who is kneeling, while the lower part of the character looks like two hands, side by side, palms extended upwards as if ready to receive something. The second character, pronounced *nuo* (rather like the English word "gnaw"), means "to consent" or "to promise."

Once we understand it this way, we can identify the two processes involved in commitment. First, we have to consent to bear a burden, and then we have to follow through with the act of making a promise. Agreeing to carry a load without the promise to carry it through to its destination isn't commitment. Only when we consent and follow through is the process of commitment complete. In fact, the simplest way to define commitment is as "doing." How many of us make a commitment and then don't follow through? For a coach, commitments without follow-through are simply verbal statements, and commitments and verbal statements are two very different things.

It is not that a person who makes a statement of commitment and does not follow through has failed to commit. They have, but to a lie. They say "yes," when really they mean "no." Let us say that our husband or wife always says they love us, but comes home late every night and habitually flirts with other people. Are they committed? Yes, to maintaining a lie. When we make a statement without taking action, in reality we are still taking action, but real commitment is taking action to produce results. A statement is the beginning of a result. And the result is the conclusion of a statement. Commitment is a measure of our standards. It shows that our actions and words are in alignment, and whether or not we are the kind of people who can follow through.

But what about simply taking action without announcing first that you intend to do so? This amounts to a fear of commitment, to an unwillingness to make a declarative statement that gives others the opportunity to evaluate us. In shunning commitment, we reveal only a lack of self-confidence. Commitment uncompleted through action destroys our credibility, but shying away from commitment robs us of the opportunity to build credibility.

Always bear in mind that commitment is a voluntary act. No one can force us into commitment. If we are unwilling to commit to something, then we should refuse to do so. But when we choose commitment, then we have a responsibility to ourselves to see it through.

## LEARNING TO COMMIT

A coach asked a student in Shenzhen who went by the English name of Sunny to complete a task by the following week.

"I can't commit to being able to do that by next week," said Sunny.

"What's the difference between making a commitment and not making a commitment?" the coach asked.

"If you make a commitment, there has to be a result," she replied.

"So, why can't you make a commitment now?"

"Well, the last time I made a commitment to do a similar thing, I didn't get it completed, so I've decided not to make commitments to do things I'm not confident I can get done."

"Last time, you made a commitment and then didn't get it done, is that right?" said the coach.

"Yes," said Sunny.

"So, you've decided it's time for a change of strategy. No more making commitments to do things you're not confident you can get done?"

"Yes, that's it."

"But what about changing the factors that produced last time's result?" the coach asked her. "You've changed from being willing to make a commitment to not being willing to make a commitment. But wouldn't it be far better to change from being unable to meet a commitment to 'I'm willing to improve myself and meet my commitments in future'?"

After all, accepting a commitment is a certain road to self-improvement.

*Self-discipline*

Commitment is about self-discipline. If we are committed to being vegetarian, we follow a strict meat-free diet. And when we commit to not becoming angry in response to others, we are disciplining our emotions. Similarly, when we say, "I want to be happy," we are making a commitment to discipline ourselves to live with a certain attitude. Whatever we commit to do – whether it is filing a company report by the next morning, or taking our children to see a movie – we have to impose discipline on ourselves to ensure it happens.

During the period of the Three Kingdoms, Zhuge Liang (181– 234) was a military commander and prime minister under King Liu Bei. His self-discipline and devotion to the king are legendary in China. In his early years he lived a simple farming life, studying by night. His reputation as a man of wisdom spread to the point that King Liu Bei visited him to seek his advice on three occasions, and in gratitude for this honor, Zhuge agreed to become the king's adviser. In a letter, written late in life, before heading an expedition of war, Zhuge Liang wrote to the king's son, "The responsibility the king has bestowed on me makes me feel anxious day and night, and I worry that I will not be up to the job and will disappoint him." Zhuge became the king's – and later the son of the king's – chief strategist, leading expeditions to the south and north, before eventually dying of overwork.

Zhuge is remembered to this day as a man who declared his intentions and then had enormous self-discipline in carrying them through. Some might think, however, that his commitment was to the king. In fact, his commitment was to himself, and he maintained it with iron self-discipline.

 *Integrity*

When we give someone our word that we will do something, we make a psychological contract with them, and they will wait for us to fulfill our side of the contract. But if our commitment stops at the statement, and we don't follow through, it is equivalent to arbitrarily tearing up the contract, and the other party will lose trust and confidence in us. A psychological contract is informal. It has many undefined terms, all of which can be changed. Say we borrow a much-loved book from a friend and promise that we will return it one week later, and then have to leave town on a trip before we have finished the book. Most of us would renegotiate with our friend so that we could keep the book a little longer. In a psychological contract, in other words, the terms of our commitment can be adjusted as long as there is discussion of the issue.

Our past actions form the basis of other people's expectations of us. It is on the basis of these past actions that people decide whether they can take us at our word. Our actions, in other words, are the basis of our integrity. When we borrow money from a bank, we are assessed on our credit rating, and much the same is true of our relationships with other people.

Integrity is an essential element in all our personal and business relationships with people. For Confucius, the man without integrity is like a cart with no axle. In Confucianism, integrity is the cornerstone of trust. As one student of Confucius put it, "The noble man can mobilize the people only when he has their trust." In a similar sense, the man of integrity who has won the trust of a king can give honest advice. Without trust, honest advice might sound like slander.

 *Focused Attention*

The legendary statesman Zhuge Liang won the respect and love of the people he governed because, throughout his life, he was focused on following through with his commitments. Shortly before his death, he made out a will. All he had to leave his family was a silk farm – despite his long years of service as prime minister, which undoubtedly provided many opportunities for him to acquire personal wealth, he had no other properties or wealth.

But how is it possible to focus our attention in such a way? Timothy Gallwey, the tennis coach who became a corporate coach, invented a formula: $P = p - i$, or "Performance equals potential minus interference." The greater the interference, the less we achieve. We all have enormous potential, but interference robs us of focus and we fail to achieve what we might. The problem, we might think, is how to recognize interference, but in fact it is not so difficult once we wake up to its presence. Any beliefs or concepts unrelated to our goals are interference. Generally, it is not outside factors that prevent us from reaching our goals, but something inner – an attitude we have, or a mistaken view of ourselves.

Any number of kinds of interference can affect commitment. An example is procrastination, where we comfort ourselves with the words, "It's all right, the other party won't mind," or self-centered judgments such as, "It's not important." These are examples of interferences that have to be eliminated if we are to follow through on our commitments. Let interference get the upper hand, and it will be difficult to follow through on any commitment. On the other hand, once we have identified interference, we have found the cause of poor performance. A coach needs to explore this in some depth with clients, in order for them to fully understand why it is that they are less focused on their commitments than they should be and why people distrust them.

Commitment is an exercise in self-discipline, but it also comes through knowing where our heart is. It is an action that follows through on a promise, and it requires focus to achieve. Remove all interferences, and we can take action on our psychological contract.

## 3. Responsibility

We tend to be much better at identifying what others should be responsible for than we ourselves. At a meeting, for example, we might say, "Let's find someone to handle this." But when we do this, we are automatically taking ourselves out of the loop. There are many

Non-Separation

Initiative          Willingness

situations where we allow someone else to take responsibility. At the end of the day, most of us are good at passing the buck, and we do it habitually.

For a coach, such behavior doesn't amount to being responsible, but is rather excuse making. There are three reasons for this. First, taking responsibility is an attitude toward life and issues. Second, taking responsibility is about realizing that responsibility centers on ourselves, and that it cannot be handed over to others. Third, all of our actions are a result of our choices, and we have to take full responsibility for all our choices; we cannot blame them on external factors.

"The disease of men is this – they neglect their own fields, and go to weed the fields of others, and what they require from others is great, while what they lay upon themselves is light." So wrote the Chinese philosopher Mencius three centuries before the birth of Christ. His point was simply that we demand far more responsibility of others than we do of ourselves. But the reality is, we are wholly responsible for ourselves. As Sartre put it, "We are our own choice." Everything we are today is a product of our choices, not of external forces. And since this is the case, we have to be responsible for our choices.

If we do not take responsibility, we are like the person who says, "My family never cared for me, and that's why I've never been a success in life," or "That's just the way I am, and there's nothing I can do about it." Such statements mark the speaker as having chosen to be a victim and as making others responsible for the way they are. Interestingly, we are quick to leap forward and prove we are right in an argument, but when it comes to questions like, "Why am I like this?" or "What will I become?", more often than not we shirk responsibility and solicit sympathy by being a victim. Victims are by definition helpless, and by choosing that role we deny ourselves power. When we passively blame external factors for the conditions of our lives, we fail to recognize the truth of our existence – that it is ours to control.

As Frankl recognized, no one can take away our ultimate freedom. What we are today, we have become by choice. We are the architects of our own lives. But freedom and responsibility are two sides of a coin. By recognizing that we freely choose, we also have to recognize that we are responsible for our choices. When we are responsible, we are conscious every moment of what we are doing, and this allows us to make important decisions and to feel in control of our lives.

Since taking responsibility is an attitude, what is the deeper meaning behind it? In coaching, we believe that the reason we are unwilling to take responsibility is because of our sense of separation from others and from things.

 ## Non-separation

The concept of "non-separation" is Buddhist, and it points to the interconnectedness of all things. Not seeing the interconnectedness of things, the Buddha taught, brings suffering and pain, and is the source of many of the world's problems. For Buddhists there is no separation between the self and others. As the classic Diamond Sutra puts it, "When you have a notion of a person, or a notion of self, or a notion of all other sentient beings, then there is separation."

For Buddhists, if we don't embrace non-separation, there can be no peace in our hearts. Separation results in polarities of action and inaction, good and bad, like and dislike. Most people's minds are unable to transcend what Buddhists call the "Six Dusts of Form," which are color, sound, scent, taste, texture, and thought, and this gives rise to feelings of separation. This may all sound somewhat abstract, but it is easy enough to see how, by seeing ourselves as separate from other people, we become judgmental. We might say, for example, "He's got shifty eyes, and I don't trust him," or "My God, have you seen how she dresses!"

## DO YOU LIKE DURIAN?

The durian – a notoriously smelly tropical fruit – is known to its fans in the Far East as the "king of fruits." But for those who cannot stand the smell, it might as well be the "devil of fruits." Tour guides in Thailand are in the habit of telling Chinese tour groups not to bring them back to their hotel for fear of upsetting the other guests.

On one occasion a client was describing one of her colleagues to her coach. Just the sight of the colleague, she explained, upset her, and she was finding it near impossible to work with the person.

After thinking for a moment, the coach asked her: "Do you like durian?"

"No," the client replied.

"Do you think it's wrong to eat durian, then?" the coach asked.

"No, of course not," the client laughed.

"That's a start. Has it occurred to you, then, that disliking someone doesn't necessarily mean there is anything wrong with them? We can dislike them and still find ways to continue to be their colleague."

Far too often, our likes and dislikes separate us from things. The judgments we make can become a form of interference that holds us back from achieving things. We can all benefit, next time we are confronted with a situation where we are tempted to retreat from something we don't like, by asking ourselves: "Do I like durian?"

The Greater Vehicle, or Mahayana, school of Buddhism teaches that to be completely free we need to accept our non-separation from others. Our essence is something we share with all other life, and it was this the Buddha was pointing to when he said, "An ordinary heart is nature, and it has no separation ... When you are hungry you eat. When you are tired you sleep. When you want love, you love. When you need to cry, you cry." An ordinary heart, in other words, is the heart of a child. The external world presses on the child, however, almost from the moment they are born, and the more we learn from that external world the greater our sense of separation grows. We begin to measure ourselves by the success of others, developing an imbalanced attitude of respecting those wealthier than ourselves and looking down on those who have less.

Non-separation is harder to grasp than it first appears, because it is the opposite of what we know. As the Buddha Maitreya put it, "Knowing how to differentiate is knowledge. Not knowing how to differentiate is wisdom." It is rather like saying, the more we know the less we can see, and the less we know the more clearly we can see. This is difficult, because our lifestyles make it impossible for us not to acquire knowledge and skills. But it is equally important for us to be able to rely on our own natures, and this is where we can find non-separation. In the *Ren* Coaching Model, internal development and external knowledge are equally important. Only through self-understanding can we achieve non-separation and start to take responsibility and enjoy the freedom of doing so.

 ## Willingness

When responsibility comes from the heart, it comes with a spirit of willingness, and this is a way of saying that responsibility is an attitude. This is something that many of us don't see clearly. We see responsibility as something that is imposed on us, and therefore we feel pressured by it. But is this real responsibility? Let's say a deadline is missed at work. An investigation is mounted, responsibility is assigned, and the person held responsible faces the consequences. This is an allocation of blame, not an issue of responsibility. We may talk about taking responsibility, but what we are really doing is determining who is right and wrong, and assessing the cause and seriousness of a mistake. True responsibility is ever present and comes from the heart.

Contrary to most of our thinking, this willing attitude of taking responsibility doesn't mean that it always results in action. We tend to think of being responsible as doing something, such as compensating the driver whose car we damaged in a motor accident that we caused. But responsibility, when it comes from the heart, is an attitude that informs everything we do in life. We have freedom to choose our lifestyles, but we have to be responsible for those choices. If we choose, say, to be a thief, we have to be responsible for the fact that we may very well end up as a prison inmate. Taking responsibility means putting responsibility on ourselves. Everything starts and ends with "I." Everything is done because we are willing. We don't complain and we don't blame others for how we choose to be. We accept everything as our responsibility.

## WHO'S XIAO WANG?

At a dinner event, a client shared with one of our coaches a story he had heard about his local basketball team.

The team was down quite a few points in a match against a rival team from another city, and had an air of defeat about them. Attempting to rally the team's morale, the coach asked them sternly, "What would Yao Ming [the famous Chinese basketball player] do if he was here now?"

"He'd fight back to turn the game around," one of the players called out.

"And what would Xiao Wang do?" the coach then asked.

"Who's Xiao Wang?" the players asked in bewilderment.

"Xiao Wang's the one who chose to give up," said the coach. "That's why you've never heard of him. How do you choose?"

The team fought back and won their game.

# Initiative

"Take a Letter to Garcia" was a story published in 1899 and later popularized by the self-help guru Dale Carnegie, whose success meant that it was translated into many languages. The story recounts how, when war broke out between the United States and Spain in 1898 over US support for Cuban insurgents fighting for independence from the Spanish colonial government, it was vitally important for the US to make contact with Garcia, the head of the Cuban insurgency. But Garcia was hidden deep in the forested mountains of Cuba, and no one knew precisely where he was. The US president was told that if anyone could find Garcia, it was a man by the name of Rowan. Sure enough, Rowan secretly made his way to Cuba by boat, disappeared into the forests for three weeks, and emerged on the other side of Cuba after a very dangerous journey, having delivered the letter.

Rowan's initiative and sense of responsibility has become legendary, and his story still lives on today. Can we take on this kind of spirit of initiative in our own lives? Wouldn't it be exhausting? The answer is: only when we regard responsibility as a burden, and only when we imagine that we always have to act on responsibility. As we have already mentioned, responsibility doesn't always equate with action. But when we willingly take initiative, our hearts are light and we don't complain. In such circumstances, we don't fear being pressured. We take our actions comfortably and naturally.

After all, the moment we say, "this has nothing to do with me," we deny our own importance – even our very existence. When we take responsibility, we have ceased being victims of our environment, and when we take initiative our sense of responsibility becomes apparent to those around us. It is a powerful force of influence.

 ## 4. Appreciation

The Chinese philosopher Laozi once said that the saint doesn't take a point of view. He looks into people's hearts, rewarding those who are good, but equally rewarding those who are evil. This strengthens the goodness of those who are good, and plants seeds of goodness in the hearts of those who are not. The saint repays both the honest person and the dishonest person with honesty.

Laozi's point was that the saint appreciates every person he comes into contact with. It is easy enough to reward good deeds and to trust trustworthy people, but to reward a bad person or trust a dishonest person is much harder. The reason is our separation from others, which causes us to judge – and judgment results equally in appreciation and disdain. Why are we so much more caring of our own children than of other people's? Simply because they are not ours. But, as the Chinese philosopher Mencius pointed out, we are all alike in being born with good natures, and the nature of a child isn't different because he or she was born to someone else. The difference lies only in our feelings and our judgments – good and bad, beautiful and ugly, like and dislike.

When we talk about real appreciation, we have to transcend these standards of value. We have to learn appreciation that transcends good or bad, and beautiful or ugly. As a Chinese saying puts it, "Sometimes a yardstick is not long enough to measure a space, and sometimes a ruler may be more than enough." When we begin to practice true appreciation, we see the advantages of both the yardstick and the ruler.

With appreciation, a leader can win hearts. The essence of modern human resources management is to put the right person in the right position, and at the heart of that there has to be appreciation. Corporations are huge collections of professionals doing everything from production and sales to marketing and finance. If we use a uniform standard to measure performance, we won't find a perfect worker, because each professional requires specific skills and each person has their own personality. Appreciation means recognizing their strengths and placing them in appropriate positions. With appreciation, it becomes easy to tap into people's talents and utilize them as effectively as possible.

Appreciation is an affirmation of others. In the Chinese classic, *The Art of War*, Sun Tzu writes: "Only when you know your enemy as well as you know yourself, can you win the battle." This is a way of saying that only by appreciating your enemies can you defeat them. If you know their strengths and weaknesses as well as you know your own, any battle can be won. Without appreciation, you will fail to see the worth of your opponents. As *The Art of War* teaches us, if we know ourselves but don't know our opponents, we will sometimes win and sometimes lose; but if we don't know ourselves or our opponents, we will lose every time.

In teamwork, appreciation is of almost unlimited value. It can stimulate passion and bring out the enthusiasm of the whole team, acting as a magnetic force in a company. We should not underestimate how quickly appreciation can spread. When leaders appreciate subordinates, appreciation leads the company. People who are appreciated have increased self-confidence, and become better at giving appreciation themselves, allowing it to spread like a chain reaction. The team becomes harmonious and the company's morale is enhanced.

*Love*

What is love? It is a question to which almost every one of us will have a different answer, so let us put that aside for a moment and think about health. Health is also a difficult thing to define, except as the non-existence of disease. Health is inherent – it is our basic nature. Love is much the same. It is inherent in us, and our ability to love is very great – particularly when we recognize the non-separation of everything; that everything is relative and not absolute, and that there is beauty in ugliness, and ugliness can be transformed into beauty.

We have many misconceptions about love. We might say that it starts with loving ourselves. When a leader tells a staff member, "I care about you, and yet you are not listening to me," the leader may well think he really cares for the person he is talking to, but the truth is that he is reprimanding them. What he really cares about is his own point of view and superiority. Appreciation out of love entails paying attention to the other person and loving his or her strengths. It is not about projecting your values on to others.

Many of us also see dependence as love. Without the person we love, we feel incomplete. Perhaps our partner is too busy with work and doesn't have enough time for us, and we find ourselves saying, "I love her so much, there's no meaning in my life without her."

This isn't love. It is passive dependence. When we are passively dependent, we are always busy looking for other people to love us, and we can end up like someone who only knows how to beg for food, and has no food to give to others. When we are like this, in our hearts there is an abyss that can never be filled, and we lose the ability to be alone. Essentially, when we do this we rely on our relationships with others to define who we are.

The only reason for love is love itself. We can "like" for many different reasons, but when we love someone, we love everything about them. If we like someone, we generally only like certain aspects of them. There is no standard in "love," but in "like" there are many. In "love," the focus is on the other person, but in "like" the focus is on ourselves.

Appreciation is something that happens through inherent love. A person who doesn't know how to appreciate has already closed her heart to love and given up the ability to love. Appreciation out of love is embracing all those who come close to you.

 ## Cherishing Ourselves and Others

Appreciation means choosing to see people's strengths and the good sides of situations. It means cherishing what we all have, and suspending judgment. It isn't about whether a person is beautiful or ugly, good or bad. Appreciation is an attitude. More than that, it is a discovery of goodness and value.

An old Chinese saying recognizes the importance of "cherishing an old broom as a precious thing." It refers to the importance of not overlooking the things in life that deserve love but which are all too often taken for granted. But this is a process that has to start with ourselves. Only when we cherish ourselves, will others appreciate us. An ancient Chinese story recounts how a man called Gong Wenxuan met a man called You Shi, and on seeing that he only had one leg asked him whether he was born that way or whether he lost his leg in an accident. You Shi replied, "I was born this way. It didn't happen later in life, and because I was born like this it has made me unique and different from ordinary people who have two legs."

You Shi clearly cherishes himself in this story, but there is another element to it. You Shi doesn't judge himself the way many other people might. He chooses instead to emphasize his uniqueness, and in cherishing uniqueness we find a standard for appreciation that doesn't judge. The statue of Venus de Milo is missing an arm, and yet we find her beautiful, and think she is perfect as she is. When we cherish uniqueness, appreciation comes naturally.

## Acceptance

Leaders who always says "no" don't know how to appreciate others, and through rejection they reveal a superiority complex. Appreciation cannot be expressed through refusal; it is expressed through acceptance. Refusal engenders feelings of failure, and makes us feel helpless. Even when we are confident, energetic, and passionate, we feel frustrated and inferior when a leader pours cold water on our ideas. Even if we pretend to put up with it, in our heart we will feel dissatisfied with and estranged from our workplace.

Appreciation is about accepting others for their uniqueness. Our natural discriminating values fall away and we find it easier to overlook others' flaws. Appreciation, in other words, boosts our tolerance levels, and enables us to avoid using rejection as a strategy for dealing with people. It is about acceptance and drawing on the strengths of others. Every one of us is happy to receive a look of appreciation, a smile, a friendly pat on the shoulder, and a word of encouragement. Acceptance is our appreciation of others' uniqueness.

 ## 5. Giving

For most of us, giving is conditional – we expect something in return. But this kind of giving is actually a form of taking. We might complain to our lover or spouse, "I've given you everything, and you give me nothing in return." We might give someone an opportunity,

and then watch them squander it. "I've done so much for you, and you don't appreciate it," we say. Such situations are common. Much of what we do is done with the expectation of taking something in return, and when we don't get it we feel like we have wasted our time.

For a coach, such feelings come about because we don't understand the real meaning of giving. Giving and taking are opposites. Like everything else we have discussed so far, they are attitudes. And when two people argue over giving and taking, they ignore the middle ground between the two. That middle ground is investment. True giving is just what it suggests – we give unconditionally, expecting nothing back. When we give with an expectation of a return, on the other hand, it cannot be classified as giving, but it can be considered an investment provided the giver and the receiver are clear that this is the case. An investment, however, comes with risk, and when we make an investment and it doesn't produce the benefits we had hoped for, we have to accept responsibility for it. If we blame the person we made the investment in, then we were neither giving nor investing – we were taking.

When we dig into our pocket for a coin and help out someone in need, we might be giving or we might be expecting a return. The difference isn't in the act of handing over the money, but in the intention. When we are focused on the person we are giving to, we are genuinely giving; but when we are looking to get something back from the person, we are looking for a return. Giving is inclusive, and we do it in a spirit of generosity. Let us say we have a valuable employee who resigns to take up another position. If we have embraced giving as an attitude, we might say to them, "I respect your decision and support it, but if you want to come back my door is open any time." Some bosses will even go to the extent of helping former employees set up their own businesses. This is true giving – a concern about the development of staff.

Taking, on the other hand, is a closed attitude that places us at the center of the universe. If this is the way we are and we hear that a valuable employee is moving on, our first thought will be our own loss. We will probably react with resentment, or even with anger. Of course, this can also work conversely: if an employee thinks only of what is in a job for themselves, they are also acting in a closed way that is focused only on immediate and evident returns.

## CHARITY AND THE CASH REGISTER

A property developer who had been trying unsuccessfully for some time to rent out space in an apartment building in Guangzhou joined the *Ren* Coaching programs. He admitted to his coach that although he had been blaming the low take-up on the fact that his apartment block wasn't particularly well located, he was also imposing a high surcharge on the rental costs of the apartments. His coach inspired him to lower the surcharge and make a lower profit on a higher turnover.

The developer returned to his office and laid out the new policy with his staff, before taking a few days off to help out with a charity that organized a series of inspirational activities for teachers, parents, and students from local schools.

On returning to his office several days later, the developer was surprised to find that the occupancy rate for the apartment building had shot up from 10% to 90% virtually overnight. His staff told him that an agent had come looking for him the same day he left the office. When they told the agent the new rates, and told him that the boss had gone off to do some charity work, the agent immediately recommended a number of his clients to look at the apartments.

Elated, the developer called his coach and said, "While I was doing that charity work, the cash registers were ringing the whole time. Can you believe it?"

Sometimes, a spirit of giving can produce unexpected results.

Many of us are constantly measuring the return on our investment, and we tend to argue about who is doing more and who is doing less. This isn't giving; it is actually a form of taking. When we are taking, we are asking, "What can you do for me?" No matter how we behave, or even how generous we may superficially appear, we are actually only focused on the benefits to ourselves. In truth, however, giving is about acting in the interests of others.

As Laozi put it, "The reason heaven and earth are enduring is because they exist not for their own ends." When we learn to embrace this form of disinterested giving, we enter a new dimension. Successful leaders are willing to give, and this is why they attract so many followers. But to understand whether we are really giving, we need to look deep into ourselves and examine whether our motives are really cloaked in selfishness.

 ## Selfishness

The force behind giving is selfishness. Why do we say that? As Laozi puts it, "The sage puts himself to the background, but is always to the fore. He remains outside but is always there. Is it not because he does not strive for any personal end that all his personal ends are fulfilled?"

For Laozi, the person who understands the *Tao*, or the *Way*, doesn't insist on putting themselves first, but in doing so wins respect and esteem. By putting others before themselves, they guarantee the security of their own lives; and by not putting their own profits and losses before those of others, they guarantee the success of their own spiritual mission. In other words, the *Tao* is selflessness, and so is giving. But, at the same time, Laozi is quick to point out that in this way the sage's "personal ends are fulfilled." The objective of selflessness, says Taoism, is to achieve self-interest. After all, at the end of the day, selfishness is our nature and the essence of our existence.

Understanding this, however, requires shifting our under-standing of the word "selfishness." For Laozi, the selfishness of the sage isn't aimed at acquiring material objects and sensual pleasures, but is a kind of spiritual aspiration. When most of us think about selfishness we think about maximizing our interests in the shortest possible time, and we focus on tangible benefits, such as a pay rise or a bigger house. But Taoist selfishness isn't the kind of self-interest that abandons all scruples and virtues for short-term benefits. As the Ming dynasty (1368–1644) interpreter of Laozi, Xue Hui, puts it, when a sage gives selflessly he doesn't think about what he will get in return, and yet in the end his self-interest is satisfied. A modern-day example that most of us can relate to is the feeling we get when we donate to a worth-while charity. We expect nothing in return, but in fact we do get something. Giving is always selfish, in this sense.

*Joy*

If even selfless giving has a long-term selfish interest, what precisely is it? Put simply, it is the feeling we have when we lavish gifts on our children. It makes us happy; it fills our hearts with joy. In short, it is the joy of giving that is born of a natural passion, and this is by no means restricted to children.

Yuan Zhen and Bai Juyi were Tang Dynasty (618–907) poets, and both lived out their lives childless. One day, Yuan wrote a letter to Bai and said how sad this made him feel. "With no offspring, does that mean our poems will go with us to the grave?" Bai's response was a poem that celebrated the joy the two poets had experienced in their lives from producing poetry. And while neither produced children, their poems have been read by countless generations and are still treasured in China to this day.

Many historical figures achieved their fame through a lifetime of giving born of their passions. The Greek mathematician, engineer, astronomer, and philosopher Archimedes (287–212 BC) is famously reputed to have run naked through the streets of Syracuse crying "Eureka!" after discovering the principles of water buoyancy while taking a bath. Despite engineering feats that are credited with saving the city of Syracuse from Roman invasions, and mathematical breakthroughs that made him probably the greatest mathematician of antiquity, he died at the hands of a Roman soldier neither rich nor famous. Similarly, Copernicus (1473–1543), who formulated the world's first helio-centric, or sun-centered, theory of the solar system, and Galileo (1564–1642), whose astronomical observations proved Copernican theory, both risked imprisonment with their controversial theories, and Galileo was indeed incarcerated late in life.

The joy of giving of ourselves might be the passion for creativity that has marked the lives of so many notable names in history, but it might also be the simple joy that all of us experience when we see the happiness that our giving produces in others. There is a very simple logic here. We are happy when the people we are with are happy, and in the process of giving to them we bring joy to ourselves.

## GIVING FOR HAPPINESS

The Chinese expression for happiness is *kuaile* (快乐), which literally means "fast happy." As always, there are hidden meanings in these Chinese characters that have been used for countless centuries. As Qian Zhongshu (1910–98), one of China's most formidable literary intellects of the 20th century, once pointed out, *kuai* (fast) *le* (happy) is a way of saying that happiness is a fleeting thing that comes as quickly as it goes.

Happiness is something we all say we long for, but how often do we really think about how to attain it? In a coaching session, a client said to the coach: "You know, I just want to be happy, but I never seem to be able to attain it. What am I doing wrong?"

"Have you thought about making other people happy first?" the coach asked. "You may well be unhappy because you're not making other people in your life happy."

Giving to attain happiness is something that we all too often forget to do. And giving to attain happiness is the same thing as saying that in order to win, we have to allow our staff, our clients, and those who are close to us to win first.

Happiness may well be a fleeting thing, but when we give we find that it can come to us just as quickly as it once left us.

## Selflessness

Giving is selflessness. When ego is involved, we are no longer giving; we are taking. When we claim, "I'm so good to him, and yet he's not good to me," does it really mean what it appears to mean? In reality, the giver is taking. Giving shouldn't be a pretext for something that is expected in return. Giving is its own reward, and the ego has no place in it.

Selflessness doesn't necessarily mean we *are* unimportant. On the contrary, we *are* important, and because of that we have the ability to give. Being important is another way of saying, "I am enough." This is the opposite of a taker, who says: "I am not enough." Only when we have attained this is there genuine selflessness. In selflessness, the other person is most important.

We all have our own goals, but there are essentially two ways to reach them. One way is to put our own interests above those of others. The other is to employ selflessness to help others to achieve their goals and in the end achieve our own – the path of mutual dividends. The objectives might be the same, but the processes differ and the end results will be profoundly different.

**6. Trust**

Trust is a slippery concept, but at heart it means two things. The first is trusting on the basis of belief. This might be based on faith, or an assertion of confidence, or simply an expectation that the person you have chosen to trust can be relied upon. It

is, in other words, a psychologically oriented definition. But another meaning of trust defines it in terms of interaction. In other words, trust is an intention or a behavior, of one person having trust in another's behavior. This is a more sociologically oriented definition. Neither definition is more correct or incorrect than the other.

But how does a coach see the issue of trust? For a start, a coach isn't interested in defining trust. What is more important is the experience of trust.

In daily life, we say things like "I think I can trust him," or "I don't think I can trust her." We might say, when disappointed, "I trusted her, but she let me down." Mantras like this are so commonplace we barely give them a second thought. Along with trust comes deceit and disappointment, and such – we tell ourselves – is life. But take a look at those statements again. They are all about the objects of our trust: "*That person* is worth trusting," or "*That person* isn't worth trusting," or "*That person* let me down." In each instance, the emphasis is on the recipient of our trust, not on ourselves. Most of us tend to do this. When we think about trust, we think about other people. But is that really the way it should be?

It doesn't seem to be the way that Zhuge Liang, the farmer turned kingly advisor turned master strategist we have already heard about, thought of trust. In a famous story in Chinese history, Zhuge Liang captured Meng Huo, the third-century leader of tribal warriors in the southern regions of the Kingdom of Shu, seven times before Meng finally conceded defeat. On every occasion but the last, Meng argued vociferously that his capture wasn't a real defeat, and Zhuge Liang set him free. The first time he was captured, Meng argued that he would never have been caught had it not been for the narrow roads he was forced to flee on. He said that he would surrender freely if he was captured a second time. The second time, he argued that he had only been captured because his own army was in mutiny, and again pleaded that he would surrender voluntarily if he was captured again. And so it went each time Meng fell into Zhuge Liang's hands. Despite the fact that Meng's arguments became increasingly preposterous, Zhuge Liang continued to set him free to lead the rebel armies of the south. It was only on the seventh occasion when he was captured that Meng broke down and swore allegiance to Zhuge Liang, promising that the southern rebels would never again rise up against the Kingdom of Shu. "You have the power of heaven," Meng told Zhuge Liang. "The people of the south won't go against you."

It is a story that has been told for centuries in China, and it is remembered because Zhuge Liang continued to offer his trust to Meng Huo, despite the fact that Meng repeatedly broke his word. Meng, in short, appeared to be completely untrustworthy, but time and again Zhuge Liang released him after capturing him, despite the advice of his generals. Zhuge Liang believed that Meng was key to stability in the southern regions. After all, Meng could rule over the southern tribes as no outsider could, and so Zhuge Liang persisted in capturing and setting Meng free until Meng had no choice but to recognize that he was up against a superior opponent. This earned Zhuge Liang Meng's respect and loyalty.

Zhuge Liang understood that trust isn't something centered in the object of trust but in the initiator. In other words, we have to give trust in order to find it. When we are the initiators of trust, the behavior of those who receive it doesn't affect us. To do otherwise is effectively to hand over our power to trust to someone else – we become passive.

## Creation

When trust is offered unconditionally, it is a form of creation. It creates new relationships, new possibilities, new ways of living life in a mutually supportive way with others. When we are trusted and it is clear what those around us expect from us, we will try very hard to live up to their expectations, and often even surpass them. In fact, there is nothing like trust to affect in a positive way the dynamics between two people and among the members of a group. It strengthens the solidarity of a business and acts as a lubricator for communication.

Without trust, we cannot talk about teamwork. Without trust, the members of a team begin to act defensively, refusing to accept criticism and concealing their weaknesses. Lack of trust breeds extreme cautiousness and an environment where everyone tries to protect themselves. Creativity beats a retreat, and eventually everyone's efforts to maintain a safe status quo affect efficiency.

Leaders who cannot trust others tend to shoulder too many responsibilities themselves. Stressed out from trying to do too much themselves, they dream of having quality staff who can lighten their load; on the other hand, they fear that quality staff will compete for their power and plot against them. Such leaders are slaves to their inability to trust and run the risk of burning out.

For both the team and the leader without trust, the workplace is like a barren field in which nothing can come into being.

 *Fearlessness*

When Zhuge Liang trusted Meng Huo, it was evidence of Zhuge's self-confidence. He had no fear of being deceived and couldn't be made a victim of Meng's deception. Zhuge Liang had no doubt that he would continue to capture Meng and win him over. If Zhuge Liang hadn't trusted himself, this would never have happened. This is the same thing as saying that when we fail to trust ourselves, we fail to trust others – and this is a manifestation of fear.

This is true of many occasions in our lives. Much of the time, when we fail to put our trust in others, it is because we are afraid to trust. We feel insecure, and fear being cheated and losing control of situations. Worse, we lack the confidence to empower our subordinates, worrying that if we share key resources with others they will become more powerful than we are and we will be left by the wayside.

Insecurity is basically a lack of self-confidence, but the two feed into each other. This vicious circle gets under way when we rely on others to determine our self-worth. We all have the psychological need to be recognized by others, but if we are not careful this need can become the sole determinant of our self-esteem, and we start relying on others to define us. When we do this, we give them the power to mold us.

When we lack security, we worry about what others think about us, and how they are going to treat us. We choose to be protective, rather than open. After all, not giving ourselves the right to trust others is a way of protecting ourselves, of keeping ourselves from harm in order to maintain our sense of security. A related need to protect ourselves may come from a sense of abandonment. But if insecurity is an internal feeling, abandonment is an internal activity. When we feel abandoned by society, it is because we have abandoned, or given up on, ourselves. We might feel abandoned by someone because they have changed, and our response is to build a wall around ourselves and refuse to trust and appreciate others. But, in reality, we all know that we cannot stop those around us from growing, and the only way to avoid being abandoned is to grow and change along with them. To do otherwise is to abandon ourselves. Like insecurity, a sense of abandonment creates fear, and if our fear exceeds our self-confidence we tend to build a wall between ourselves and others, resulting in an inability to extend trust.

Fearlessness is an external manifestation of a deep ability to extend trust. Only when we are absolutely certain about ourselves and have no fear will we be able to tear down the defenses we have built against trusting others and enjoy the possibilities that come as a result.

## DON'T FEAR FAILURE

In 2001, during knock-out rounds of the 2002 World Cup, China's chief soccer coach, Bora Milutinovic, was asked by reporters whether he was worried that he might lose his "rice bowl" – the Chinese expression for a steady job – if the team didn't make it through. He replied: "Losing your rice bowl is part and parcel of life."

The result? China qualified for the World Cup for the first time in the history of the sport.

By contrast, one client who joined the *Ren* Coaching program, told his coach that when he first went into business, he was always raring to go and willing to take risks, but once he became successful he adopted a less adventurous attitude and began to avoid taking risks.

"You don't want to take risks because you're afraid of failure," the coach said.

The entrepreneur admitted this was true, saying: "Even losing a little bit of money in a mahjong game makes me uneasy these days."

"Have you ever considered that the fact that you have only made $1 million rather than $10 million might be a form of failure?"

It is true that when we never take risks or accept challenges we keep failure at bay, but for those who do – and who are confident of their abilities – failures are just stepping-stones on the road to eventual success.

 ## Relinquishing Control

Trust isn't a concept; it is an experience. A concept can be defined in different ways, but experience is direct, and difficult to deceive ourselves about. Certain situations and people may make us feel uncomfortable, and when we are uncomfortable our experience tells us not to trust them. On the other hand, when we feel comfortable, our experience is telling us to trust.

Trust is similar to responsibility and giving – offering it doesn't necessarily get us anything in return. This is something we often fail to realize, and we fall into the trap of making our trust conditional. "If you do this," we say, "then we'll trust you." Or we say, "I trust you, so you have to do this," or perhaps, "If you don't do this, you don't trust me." This is a form of passivity, when in fact trust is about choice. We determine trust. Only *we* determine whether or not we will trust, and on what basis we choose to do so. Only once we understand this, do we have freedom of choice and are no longer simply being reactive.

Distrust, on the other hand, is a form of control. When we mistrust others, we have a powerful need to control everything, and it is only through controlling behavior that we feel secure. Controlling leaders are unable to trust their employees, and it is only when their work meets the leaders' standards that they will gradually begin to extend trust. But this is counterproductive, as controlling behavior increases the cost of management and reduces work efficiency.

Leaders who trust others start by trusting themselves, and when they extend that trust to others they relinquish control. Leaders who relinquish control trust their staff to do their jobs to the best of their ability and to solve problems. There are risks inherent in trusting others, but we have the freedom to choose our level of risk. Bold leaders start out trusting 100%, and it is only when those they trust repeatedly perform badly that they start to lower the level of trust percentage point by percentage point.

##  7. Win-win

In chess, there are three possible outcomes: I win, you lose; I lose, you win; or stalemate. Our human environment is far more complex than a chessboard, however, and many more outcomes are possible. In the marketplace, or in a relationship, it is

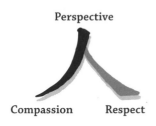

possible that both parties might lose, or that both might win. When the latter happens, we are talking about a win-win situation. When two parties win and a third party also wins, we are talking about a scenario with "multiple winners."

Leaders who are not awake to the advantages of win-win strategies throw all their efforts into crushing their opposition, to eliminating their rivals in the marketplace. Price wars are the perfect example of this. In theory, they are a win-lose strategy. Company X announces a 10% cut in prices, and Company Y reciprocates. The theory – if, indeed, there is one – behind this is that sooner or later someone will be hurting too badly to continue the fight and a winner will emerge. But the reality is that both companies lose.

More and more businesses are realizing that price wars and other strategies aimed at eliminating rivals from shared markets are lose-lose strategies. For a better understanding of how win-win situations come about, the main conceptual framework is Game Theory, a branch of applied mathematics that was first developed by the Hungarian-born mathematician and polymath John Von Neumann, and further developed by John Nash, the mathematician who was the subject of the movie *A Beautiful Mind*. Game Theory is used to analyze how players in any situation can work to maximize returns, and a classic example of how this works is the so-called Prisoner's Dilemma.

Simplifying the classic scenario somewhat, two prisoners are incarcerated in separate cells and have no way of communicating with each other. The district attorney has enough evidence to jail both of them for one year, but if he can manage to have one betray the other, or both of them to betray each other, he can impose a lengthier sentence. So the attorney offers each man a deal: if either cooperates and provides evidence about the other, his jail term will be reduced to three months, while the other's term will be 10 years. If both betray the other, they will both get jail sentences of two years.

The dilemma here is obvious. The prisoners are in a situation that offers a strong incentive for each to betray the other. The best possible outcome for either prisoner is a three-month sentence, but neither can know whether the other won't cooperate, with the result that the original one-year sentence they would have received if both had remained silent becomes a two-year sentence. Meanwhile, remaining silent runs the risk that the other will cooperate and a one-year sentence will become a 10 year sentence. For both to win, neither should put the other in a losing situation – "I win, you lose" or "you win, I lose." In a worst-case scenario, both confess and end up in a "lose-lose" situation. This is called a Nash balance, or an uncooperative balance.

Having an attitude of, "If I can't do it, then you can't do it either" inevitably results in lose-lose outcomes in which everyone has to share the losses. In other words, the thinking, "I win, you lose" is a "zero-sum" game. When we choose a win-lose strategy and only consider our own interests, the end result is a Nash balance and everyone ends up losing. The Nash balance teaches us that cooperation benefits us in the end. This conforms to the biblical tenet of "Do unto others as you would have them do unto you." Confucius followed the same logic when he advised, "Do not pass on to others what you do not want for yourself." This is a win-win strategy, a way of achieving goals through considering the interests of everyone involved.

It is impossible today for any single business to succeed in a marketplace alone. Companies, suppliers, distributors, and

## WRESTLING VERSUS THE TANGO

A client named Mai Guangfan started a restaurant in Zhongshan, a leafy city of parks in Guangdong province. Business grew far faster than he could ever have anticipated, and before he knew it he had a chain of dozens of restaurants. In fact, he liked to joke that he was opening restaurants faster than he could get around to putting the branch phone numbers on his name cards.

The key to his success, he said, was the early realization that he would have to do things differently from other Chinese restauranteurs, who typically ran their businesses in a hands-on manner, with their wives working the cashier and an uncle and aunt or two running around buying supplies from the markets.

"I had to turn to modern management methods, because I wanted to grow," said Mai.

"I believe in the science of management. I have to; otherwise, where am I going to find dozens of wives to be the cashiers in the dozens of restaurants I own?"

What is more, Mai took the highly unusual step in China of providing incentives to his management team in the form of equity – to the point that he gave up 50% of his stake in the company.

"If I hadn't given away 50%, the other 50% could have become worthless anyway," he said. "My previous bosses were unable to understand this rationale, so that's why I decided to strike out on my own."

Mai Guangfan's win-win approach is exactly what coaching promotes, and the thinking is simple: If your subordinates are competent enough to manage themselves, and you are unable to satisfy their needs in terms of salary and personal development, it is entirely possible that they will walk out on you and become powerful rivals instead.

One way a coach might put this to someone who was still having problems seeing the necessity of giving away so much could be to ask them to imagine a wrestling match. To be sure, one of the wrestlers will lose, but the winner will suffer a great deal of pain too. But let us imagine not a wrestling match, but a tango, where competition is replaced by a smooth back-and-forth collaboration.

That is what coaching means by a win-win situation.

advertising agencies all depend on each other, and this is increasingly the case as economic globalization hastens. Meanwhile, the rise of the Internet has extended the reach of businesses to every corner of the world, making cooperation ever more essential. In the midst of this competitive environment, leaders who embrace win-win strategies allow for a consolidation of power, turning resistance into cooperation and benefits all round.

 *Perspective*

If asked who is more important in a company, the receptionist or the general manager, most of us will answer "the manager." But this is to neglect the importance of the receptionist. The receptionist, after all, is the point of contact between the customers and clients and the company. A company with a bad receptionist can only lose. This isn't to say that receptionists are more important than managers; it is simply a reminder that leaders neglect the importance of lower-level staff at their own risk. Every piece, no matter how small, is an essential part of the whole. Clerks might inhabit the lower echelons of the corporate structure, but they are still essential to the daily running of business.

Much of Chinese philosophy is pervaded by the idea that there is oneness between man and nature. This is another way of saying that the universe is a single system, but to see this we all need to step back. Mencius wrote that when Confucius ascended Mount Dong, he was struck by the fact that his home province of Shandong was very small, but when he climbed Mount Tai, he realized that the Chinese empire was very small. In other words, the higher we climb, the more expansive our vision becomes. Leaders who view their companies close up only see their business, but when they step back they see a market. By standing tall we gain perspective and see the connectedness of everything. This allows us to break through the "I" in our thinking, and move from "I win" to win-win.

## Respect

Working for win-win situations requires an acceptance that we are all equal, and equality is the result of an equal measure of respect for ourselves and respect for others. "If a king regards his courtiers as brothers, they will see him as flesh and blood," wrote Mencius. "If the king regards his courtiers as he would his dogs and horses, they will see him as their ruler. If the king regards his courtiers as a field of scattered grass, they will see him as their enemy." In other words, respect breeds respect.

Respect means not imposing our will on others, and reaching a proper understanding of what is entailed in mutual respect. By communicating our notions of respect to each other, we are respecting each other. This process of communication is based on our own sense of self-respect – of not giving up and letting others decide things for us. When we respect others, we don't force them to do what they don't want to do; and when we respect ourselves, we don't allow others to force us to do what we don't want to do. These are the conditions for a win-win situation.

But another precondition for mutual respect is that there is respect for the terms of cooperation that are built up through communication. In a win-win situation, all the parties are connected by respect for what has been discussed. This is the only way to avoid situations in which one party feels that the other party is benefiting more from an arrangement and to ensure that a win-win outcome is enduring.

 ## Compassion

Compassion is opening ourselves up to the differences between people, looking at issues from others' points of view, and being considerate of them. As Confucius put it, "Noble men may differ in views but they are in harmony, while the ignoble share similar views and are in disharmony." When we live with a high degree of consideration for others, we accept those around us and maintain good interpersonal relationships.

Naturally, compassion alone isn't enough to bring about a win-win situation, but it is an important part of the quotient.

In management, there is a tendency for leaders to be either people-oriented or task-oriented. People-oriented leaders are compassionate and understanding, and aim to provide a work environment in which people feel comfortable and satisfied. Task-oriented leaders make goal achievement their priority, and they aim to create high-efficiency work environments. The leader who aims to bring about a win-win situation looks to fuse these two approaches.

 ## 8. Enrollment

Enrollment, as we use it in the Nine-Dot Leadership Model, is the opposite of "recruitment." When we recruit people, we say to them, "I want you." But when we enroll people, we attract them and inspire a spirit of voluntarism in the workplace.

Dream

Inspiration    Manifestation

Attracting talent means setting an example and establishing a calling. In the *Ren* Coaching Model, a spirit of enrollment is defined as stimulating people's dreams and rousing them to take action willingly. Inspiration is the driving force that puts a team into action. In ancient China, the sages incessantly enrolled people, and from a coaching perspective it is possible to see enrollment as a central theme of the *Four Books*, which are the cornerstone of a classic Confucian education. For instance, in *The Analects*, Confucius says: "He who exercises government by means of his virtue may be compared to the north polar star, which keeps its place and all the stars turn towards it."

Confucius would have understood the notion that being a leader is like attracting disciples. It can be easy for us to come to the conclusion that leadership is about wielding power, or throwing money at people, or even perhaps lying to people, but this isn't true leadership. When we use such "strategies," at best we are being a manager, and at worst a despot. Real leadership is the power of enrollment, and leadership is manifested through enrollment. The language may look archaic and somewhat stiff, but this is what Confucius means when he says of the perfect leader, "Let him preside over the people with gravity, then they will revere him. Let him be filial and kind to all, then they will be faithful to him. Let him advance the good and teach the incompetent, then they will eagerly seek to be virtuous."

Enrollment, however, isn't necessarily only the power to attract talent to our side. It can also simply be the power to inspire from afar. Consider Jack Welch, who was named "Manager of the Century" by *Forbes* magazine in 1999. Most corporate executives may never have met him, but that doesn't prevent them from worshiping his management style. Why? Welch has inspired countless other executives to transform themselves and to think big.

Enrollment is the ability to influence and change attitudes, and to stimulate people to act willingly. In this sense, it is the opposite of giving commands. Giving orders is a manifestation of power, while enrollment is about inspiration. Leadership studies broadly divide leadership into authoritative influence and non-authoritative influence. Authoritative influence is enforced through compulsory means, and once an order is given, there is no room for discussion. Willingly or not, it has to be carried out. That absence of consent may mean that things get done, but it is also likely to breed resentment. Non-authoritative leadership, on the other hand, leads by example and inspires an atmosphere of voluntarism.

We should not, however, confuse enrollment with persuasion. Persuasion can too easily become a form of pleading – imploring people to shift their attitudes and actions in a certain direction – because it is mostly a form of verbal guidance. Enrollment, on the other hand, often doesn't require words because it is inspirational. Take the example of a Chinese TV commercial that featured a child who sees his mother washing his grandmother's feet. The child runs to get a basin of water and brings it to his mother and announces he wants to take over. Without a word and without any persuasion or deliberate suggestion, the mother has unintentionally enrolled her child by her own actions.

We cannot persuade or command people to change their attitudes; we can only enroll them. But if it stops here, the enrollment process isn't yet complete. Enrollment is about stimulating dreams, but dreams that are not acted upon are just that – dreams. This is where leadership enrolls action, not through commands or compulsory means, but by inspiration to join in a meaningful game. Enrollment is a driving force that allows teams to play a win-win game, and it is the light that guides the team forward.

 ## Dreams

The first step in enrollment is to discover the dream. Sometimes that dream might be something extremely obvious and simple, as in the old Chinese story of Prince Cao Cao, leader of the Kingdom of Wei (220–265), whose troops ran out of water in the desert while on an expedition. In order to inspire them to march on, the prince told the troops there was a plum orchard ahead. The story is probably not true, but everyone in China knows how the soldiers salivated at the thought of the plums and continued their march. The dream of an end to their thirst inspired them to efforts they didn't think they were capable of, and even though they found no plums they were able to continue their march to the next available source of water. The reputation of Prince Cao Cao is as a despot, and the story of the plums is often used to illustrate "consoling people with false hopes," but it neatly illustrates the point that if we want people to change their behavior, we have to touch their hearts.

In terms of coaching, there are two forms of enrollment. The first is when our dreams are stimulated so that we voluntarily pursue them, and the person who enrolls us plays no part in the actual process of pursuing the dream. Think of parents who actively involve themselves in inspiring their children to take up university courses that complement their goals, even though it is the children themselves who have to undergo the coursework. This is different from the kind of enrollment where a leader's grand vision enrolls the efforts of others to achieve that vision. In this second kind of enrollment, the person who inspires is part of the process.

Coaching is about the first mode of enrollment. A coach enrolls the client to recognize their real worth, define their dreams, outline their life goals, and take action to effectively achieve them. Leaders, on the other hand, enroll others in tirelessly pursuing a common dream. If Sun Yat-sen, the father of modern China, hadn't had a grand dream of a free and independent China, there would not have been the Republican revolution of 1911 that toppled the Qing dynasty.

Clearly, the starting point for enrollment is a firm belief in our dreams, a belief that inspires and becomes a rallying point for others, who together bring the dream closer to reality. This process is also the process of the Nine-Dot Leadership Model. When we have a dream, we have passion and commitment. We embrace responsibility and appreciate everyone around us. We offer unstinting trust and adopt a win-win attitude. With this we find yet more passion, enrolling yet more people, creating new possibilities.

 *Manifestation*

We become willing to adapt our behavior when we can see the advantages of doing so from observing other people's experiences. We hope to share that experience, and we become enthusiastic about enrolling. For Confucius, the leader with a good moral character has no need to give orders, as others follow him naturally; but if he lacks moral character, even the orders he gives won't be obeyed. This is the limitless power of example.

Let us say an executive announces, "Our goal is to transform this company into the kind of place where every employee is respected by outsiders simply because they work here." He is enrolling his staff. But if he makes the announcement but then does nothing further, doubts will set in and before long, no matter how hard he tries, he will no longer be able to enroll his staff. Manifestation, in other words, is at the heart of enrollment. If we return to the story of Prince Cao Cao, under the circumstances he can be forgiven for tricking his troops into believing there was a plum orchard just ahead – they were thirsty and close to revolt. However, his story was without manifestation, and if he were to try it for a second time he would enroll no one.

## Inspiration

Whether it is stimulating one person's ideals, or stimulating collective ideals, the basic condition of success is that others are willing to embrace the ideal and to turn it into action. And the most effective way to do that is through inspiration. Generating a spirit of enrollment is an attitude and an internal ability – a force of charisma – but its external expression is a force of inspiration.

The Chinese-language *Contemporary Chinese Dictionary* defines "inspiration," or *qifa* (啟发), "as guiding others to a state of understanding." This is a little more subtle than the usual English definitions of the word, but it is not so hard to understand. Inspiration, in this Chinese sense, is a form of guidance that promotes understanding, because it is through understanding of the self that attitudes change and it becomes possible to pursue ideals. If our minds are confused and in a state of conflict, it is impossible for us to embrace an ideal and be willing to turn it into action.

In other words, if enrollment is a force that shines through belief and conviction, inspiration is the active follow-up that clears others' minds of the confusion that is standing in the way of their becoming part of the mission. Through inspiration, we can help others to identify their dreams and express those dreams outwardly. We can enroll them to take action and join us on a journey. Although it should be carried out with a spirit of equality, it is also about putting others first. After all, this is what enrollment is all about – stimulating the dreams of others.

 ## 9. Possibilities

What is impossible in life? For most of us, it is the things we cannot imagine or the things we think we couldn't possibly attain. What is possible in life? Most of us would say, the things we have already attained,

Nothingness

Inquiry          Humility

or the things we are confident of attaining. Broadly speaking, these are the limits of possibility that most of us embrace.

When we think about possibilities, we should think about our own perceptions of what is possible and what is not. And these perceptions are determined by our beliefs.

Long ago, in the state of Jin (265 - 420), a county magistrate named Le Guang invited a close friend, Du Xun, to his home for a drink. These were turbulent times in which even friends mistrusted one another. Le Guang and Du Xun sat in the living room and Le

Guang poured two glasses of wine. On the wall hung a red bowl, and as Du Xun raised his glass to his lips a shaft of sunlight penetrated the window and fell on the bow, and its reflection shimmered in the wine. Du Xun paused with the wine close to his lips, his stomach knotted with fear. It looked like a tiny red snake was floating in his glass. Le Guang, oblivious to what Du Xun thought he was seeing, raised his glass high and proposed a toast to their friendship. Unable to refuse, Du Xun gulped back his wine and the two fell into conversation.

Du Xun stumbled home that evening feeling unwell, and the next morning he felt no better. As the days passed he felt worse and worse. Nothing he took made him feel better, and the doctors he visited were at a loss to diagnose his illness. When Le Guang heard that his friend was ill, he went to visit him, and Du Xun confessed that he had been sick ever since he drank that glass of wine with a tiny snake in it. Le Guang had no idea what his friend was talking about until several days later he saw a shaft of sunlight light up the bow on his living-room wall and made the connection. He hurried to Du Xun, brought him to his house, and again poured a glass of wine to show him how the snake was in fact simply a reflection. Du Xun was miraculously cured of his illness.

In the story of Le Guang and Du Xun there are two possibilities. The first is that Du Xun drank a snake and became ill; the second is that he drank the reflection of the bow and thought he was ill. But the important thing is what Du Xun thought he saw, and the belief that grew of it. Beliefs, after all, come from what we think we have seen, the experiences we have had, and how we interpret them to ourselves. And the beliefs we hold, based on our past experiences, are what determine what we think is possible and what is not.

What we believe to be true, as in the case of Du Xun, may be untrue. But when we believe strongly that it is the case, we will let that belief govern our state of being and guide us in a false direction. Such beliefs can be enormously stubborn, and may make it difficult for us to adapt to change of any kind. In fact, at any given moment, there are infinite possibilities, but they can only be apparent when we are willing to abandon our existing beliefs. Possibilities are like water, which can take on infinite forms – in a cup, it takes on the form of a cup; in a river, it takes on the form of a river and flows to the sea, where it takes on the form of the sea.

In fact, life is like water – it is fluid and ever changing. It is limited only by our beliefs, by the possibilities we can see in any given situation. Let us say that someone reprimands us. Our usual emotional reaction is anger and the desire to reproach them back. Our past experience has taught us to respond in kind to anger, to adopt an eye-for-an-eye approach to conflict. But it is equally possible to smile at another person's anger, which in the end is only an expression of emotional exasperation.

In short, we are limited by our tendency to limit the possibilities in a situation. For many of us, our beliefs rest on a bedrock of impossibilities. When we confront a new challenge, our reaction is: "I don't know anything about this, and I can't possibly do it." This is a fixed idea that denies us the right to explore. When we build a cause-and-effect relationship between "I haven't done this before" and "I can't do it," we cannot accomplish anything in life. Cause-and-effect thinking of this kind is a kind of fatalism. "I was born into a poor family, and I can never be successful," we think, or "I'm short, and so no one will respect me." In a sense, there is a logic to such thought patterns, but in another sense they simply doom us to failures that we can blame on things outside of ourselves. "It's not that I'm not willing to work hard," we say. "It's that I was forced to be this way."

When we break through such beliefs, we create possibilities for ourselves. As Viktor Frankl says, "Everything can be taken from a man but one thing; the last of human freedoms – to choose one's attitude in any given set of circumstances, to choose one's own way." We can choose an attitude that embraces possibilities, and when we do so we have the power to set our own direction.

*Nothingness*

To embrace possibilities, we need to abandon models, strip away boundaries, and look to nothingness. To understand this, we need to think of nothingness not so much as a void but as space that allows us infinite room for movement. As Laozi puts it in *The Tao and Its Power*, "The Way is like an empty vessel, that yet may be drawn from, without ever needing to be filled." An empty cup, after all, is more useful than a full cup.

For Taoists, this sense of nothingness is a place of complete flexibility in which we do not cling to any fixed notions. As *The Tao and Its Power* puts it, "To remain whole, be twisted. To become straight, let yourself be bent. To become full, be hollow. Be tattered, that you may be renewed. Those that have little, may get more. Those that have much, are but perplexed." When we stand with a strong viewpoint – as the word itself suggests – our gaze is narrowed, and there is much that we don't see. The same is true of beliefs. And Buddhism, like Taoism, recognizes this when it urges us not to be attached to ideas. When we are faced with the confusion of external reality and remain detached, say the Buddhists, we can do so with a calm heart. We have embraced nothingness. As the Heart Sutra says, "Form is empty; emptiness is precisely form. Form is indistinguishable from emptiness and emptiness is indistinguishable from form."

When a coach talks about nothingness, he means to let go of the past, to let go of our existing beliefs, views and judgments, to adjust our attitudes and start from scratch. In this way, the client can move beyond their past experience and open their life to new possibilities.

 *Humility*

When we hang on to past experience, we are trapped in a place that provides us with limited vision. We think we have seen everything and that it is all running exactly according to the way in which we perceive it. But consider the following four statements:

"I know."

"I don't know."

"I know what I don't know."

"I don't know what I don't know."

The first is an expression of a limiting world view; a point of view dictated by fixed belief patterns. The last three statements are expressions of humility. Humility is like environmental protection for our hearts. It eliminates pollutants and establishes an inner harmony, creating infinite space in which to learn and develop. And a path of continual learning, as Confucius understood, is the only path to wisdom: "One who loves to learn is close to wisdom." In *The*

*Doctrine of the Mean,* a similar point is made: "Only when a person has traveled far and climbed high will he be humble."

 *Inquiry*

When we think we have seen everything, and we know everything there is to know, we are trapped in the past and become arrogant and defensive, blind to new possibilities. To be humble, we have to throw off the past and consider the present our starting point for everything. With humility we can say, "This is where I am now, and I am looking for a solution and plan for my future life." This is a position from which infinite possibilities arise.

# Postscript:
## It's All about
# VISION

It started with Eva's dream.

Eva had a dream of taking to China the fledgling coaching industry that had changed her life.

In 1995, she was operating out of a tiny office on Luard Road in Wanchai – Hong Kong Island's low-rent sister to Central, and once the setting for Richard Mason's *The World of Suzie Wong*. In those days, Eva was a one-woman show. In the beginning, she spent most of her time running around meeting people and working the phone.

The office was on the seventh floor, and downstairs was a cluster of traditional Cantonese teashops, where the staff of the various offices in the building would take lunch. The earliest coaching courses – all run by Eva with some part-time help – were held in the same building, and gradually, as the word spread and more and more clients began to troop in and out, the neighbors started to become curious about the streams of people who were taking courses from an outfit with the odd name of TopHuman. Slowly, the building's occupants started to drop in to find out more, and then to sign up. After I joined TopHuman in 1996, we used to joke that we converted that entire building to the cause of coaching.

At the time, coaching was a very new concept, even in North America where it began, let alone in Hong Kong, where it was essentially an unknown quantity. The International Coaching Federation was only founded in 1995 – the same year TopHuman was set up in Hong Kong – and in those early days there were just 100 members worldwide. But despite the fact that the entire industry was in its infancy, Eva was determined to take it into China.

Our first step in that direction was to open an office in Macau, still at that time a Portuguese colony, in 1996. "We knew that, if we were really going to tackle China, we needed a foothold there." Eva decided that, for the move to have any symbolic value, she was going to have to be in China before the handover of Hong Kong, which was looming on July 1, 1997.

If Hong Kong had been difficult in the very early days, China was much harder. No one had a clue what coaching was. In China, training of any kind involved a lecturer speaking to a class. But what we were proposing to do was interactive, experiential. It was a whole new category of experience, and we made countless presentations to bewildered Communist Party officials in a myriad of departments in pursuit of a corporate license. At first we took the show to Beijing because it seemed to make sense for us to start our operations in the capital. But we soon realized that we were so small it didn't really matter where we started. Next we trooped to Shanghai, before deciding – as we should have in the beginning – that with our Cantonese-speaking staff, the simplest solution was to launch coaching in China from Guangzhou, the provincial capital of Hong Kong's neighboring Guangdong province. So in 1996 we headed to Guangzhou and set up a representative office. It was still a close call in terms of getting our China business operational, because it wasn't until June 1997 – just one month before the handover – that we actually ran our first course in China.

For me, Guangzhou was the perfect solution. Southern China's leading city is a world away from Beijing's corridors of power, and an easier place to quietly start up a business – after all, it was where China's doors to the international business community first began to inch open in the late 1970s. Since graduating from university I had worked in China trading, while Eva had worked as a commercial officer at the Canadian Embassy. If there was one thing we knew about China, it was: don't move too quickly. As the Chinese saying goes, "The gun shoots the bird at the head of the flock." There are many sayings with a similar theme; another warns: "The big tree takes the brunt of the wind." They all amount to the same thing: stand up too quickly, and you will come under scrutiny. Our policy from the beginning was to take it slowly, to be low key. It stood us in good stead.

That first course we ran in Guangzhou had just one mainland Chinese on the enrollment list. The rest of the clients were Hong Kong and Macau Chinese based in China. In fact, people were skeptical about whether we could attract mainland Chinese clients at all. For a start, we were doing something that no one had attempted before, and on top of that we were charging a lot of money for it. A four-day coaching course cost 3,800 yuan (US$475), which was outrageous in China, where the typical cost for a four-day training course was 300 yuan (US$37). We took what we saw as a righteous position, and charged the same price we had been charging in Hong Kong, because – we argued, mostly to ourselves – to do otherwise would be holding the mainland Chinese in lower regard. People thought we were crazy. But the numbers of our local clients grew with every course, and within a year we had more of them than we did expatriate Chinese.

It helped that the first mainland Chinese who joined our course in Guangzhou worked for a foreign joint venture as a headhunter.

After completing the course, he started to introduce his corporate clients to us. Local advertising companies, which tend to be more adventurous, also got wind of us and began to dispatch their staff for coaching, and gradually the media started to sit up and take notice. As more and more high-caliber Chinese joined our courses, we started to attract people from elsewhere around China – in particular, from Shenzhen, Hong Kong's neighboring colossus, which had emerged as a metropolis from the rice paddies in the space of two decades. Suddenly our plans changed. We thought we would be heading to Beijing or Shanghai next, but in 1998 we found ourselves setting up a second China office in Shenzhen.

Even so, and despite the fact that Shenzhen is next-door to Hong Kong, this presented us with a problem. From the beginning, we had run all our courses in Cantonese, but in Shenzhen this was simply no longer an option. Shenzhen is a city of around 10 million immigrants who hail from every corner of China, and from the start it was obvious that we would have to start teaching in Mandarin. The thing was, apart from Eva, virtually no one on our staff spoke Mandarin. In the old days in Hong Kong, when you asked someone if they spoke Chinese, you really meant, did they speak Cantonese? Mandarin was a foreign language. Even I spoke it very badly. So, in the beginning, Eva was doing all the coaching in Shenzhen, and we were feverishly transferring our technology to our local clients.

In other words, manpower was already becoming an issue. For the China market, it was essential that we recruit local coaches and assistant coaches, but we were the only people in the entire market able to train them. We were essentially inventing the wheel – building both our market and our staff – wherever we went. To become an assistant coach typically takes around six months, and if you do another six months of assistant coaching and further coursework you can become a coach. To become a trainer – that is, someone who teaches people to become coaches – takes three years.

This became an issue when we finally decided to open an office in Shanghai. Before we did anything else, we had to go to Shanghai, recruit 10 staff, and bring them down to Shenzhen, where we put them through a six-month coaching program. Of course, we can hire secretaries, human resources people, and so on without doing this, but in Shanghai we needed more than that. Unlike in Guangzhou and Shenzhen, where we could always bring in resources from Hong Kong, in Shanghai we needed our own resources. For our staff to provide after-sales service and to liaise with clients about continuing courses, they need to be part of the coaching process.

We opened an office with 15 staff in Shanghai in 2000, and business was slow at first. But, as in Guangzhou, before long it was growing steadily. The unique thing about coaching is that it creates the need for a dialog, and this generates business. People who have done the courses need to have others around them do the courses so that they can continue the internal dialog they have started themselves. It is a word-of-mouth process and we are managing the conversation. Once someone has been through the courses, they come back as an assistant and they continue to learn. It is an after-sales service for them, but for us they become a resource. It is a win-win situation.

In Shanghai we began to standardize our operations so that all classes in China are now taught in Mandarin. The idea is that once you have signed up for a course, you can do it wherever you like. Some businesspeople take the courses because it is a good opportunity to meet other businesspeople, and someone from, say, Beijing might choose to do the course in Chengdu because they want to do business there.

In 2002, we registered an office in Beijing. That wasn't exactly our most memorable year, as we had to struggle through a cash-flow crunch in our southern operations that nearly bankrupted the company, but we came through it and continued to grow.

Indeed, though it may sound like our growth in China has been one success story after another, it has not always been so easy. We have had to overcome a myriad of difficult challenges, just as any startup company – especially one pioneering a new field of thinking in a developing market – has had to. Eva and I have often discussed why TopHuman has been a success in China when so many other companies – particularly in recent years – have borrowed our model and failed. The only thing we could come up with is that we live the model we have taken to China. The *Ren* Coaching Model is about having passion. And, as we teach in the Nine-Dot Leadership Model, with passion comes commitment, and with commitment comes responsibility for and appreciation of everything around us. With appreciation comes giving, which inspires trust and generates win-win situations. A win-win situation fires passion, and an enthusiasm for enrollment. It is not about making money, even though we are doing so. The *Ren* Coaching Model is about exploring our potential and sharing it with others.

We see it as having a sense of vision. Some people might see the "vision thing" as spin, a pie-in-the-sky concept. But there is more to it than that. It is all very well to be pragmatically focused on making money, but what happens when the business goes south? Without vision, you quit. Successful businesses are tenacious; they stick at things. That tenacity comes from vision. We came to China with a vision of what coaching could do for the country we call home, and that vision is unchanged today.

**Lawrence Leung**

# Index

## A

*A Discourse on Heaven,* 15
action through inaction, 28
adaptive leadership, 56, 186,
    187, 189-191
Aigo, 41, 42, 50
*Analects,* 25, 260
Anyang, 30
Apple, 100
appreciation, 47, 195-198,
    208, 226-232, 280
Archimedes, 238

## B

Bai Juyi, 238
behavior patterns, 89, 201
Beijing, 30-32, 42, 45, 86, 91,
    115, 161, 275, 277, 279
Buddha, 26, 219, 221, 222
Buddhism, 23, 24, 26-31, 36,
    221, 270

## C

Canon, 25, 100
Center for Public Leadership,
    187
*Chan,* 23
Chen Baofang, 44, 46
China Central Television, 45
China's National People's
    Congress, 155, 164
coaching-style listening, 58
commitment, 57, 99, 150, 190,
    195-198, 209-217, 264,
    280
communicative culture, 49
Confucianism, 24, 27, 29-31,
    36, 215
Confucius, 24-26, 28, 36, 171,
    172, 177, 198, 215, 253,
    257, 258, 260, 264, 271
corporate coaching, 12, 20, 21,
    51, 63
Cultural Revolution, 208

# D

Dalong Chemical Fertilizer Co., 67
delusional behavior, 204
Deng Xiaoping, ix, xii
Diamond Sutra, 219
*Doctrine of the Mean*, 171, 172, 199, 209, 272
Dongguan, 102, 107, 116, 141, 145, 147, 149, 151, 153
Du Xun, 266-268

# E

enrollment, 196-198, 259-266, 276, 280
experiential exercises, 3, 149

# F

Feng Jun, 41, 50
Focus Media, 45, 47
*Four Books*, 260
Frankl, Viktor, 203, 269

# G

Galileo, 239
Gallwey, Timothy, 20, 23, 216

Game Theory, 252
Gandhi, Mahatma, 200
getting personal, 15
giving, 8, 22, 56, 73, 76, 102, 128, 136, 157, 164, 191, 196-198, 201, 208, 228, 232-241, 247, 249, 255, 258, 261, 280
Golden Week, 94, 96, 97
*Guangya Shigu*, 179
Guangzhou, 3, 101, 115, 116, 160, 234, 275, 276, 278
Guatama, Siddhartha, 26
Guidu Department Store, 83-87

# H

Harvard University, 20, 187
Heart Sutra, 270
Heifetz, Ronald A. , 187
Heilongjiang, 3, 67, 68, 80
Herrigel, Eugen, 23
Hong Kong, 3, 27, 32, 52, 100, 116, 141, 194, 273-278
Huabao Electronics, 100
Huang Qijun, 51, 57
Huaqi, 42
human resources, 65, 123,

163, 167, 189, 227, 278
human touch, 9, 15, 37
human-capital program, 91

**I**

Il Giornale, 180
*In Search of Excellence*, 183
inner self, 172, 174-177
innovative thinking
    workshops, 139
International Coaching
    Federation, 274

**J**

John F. Kennedy School of
    Government, 187

**K**

key performance indicators,
    151
KFC, 118
Kingdom of Shu, 243, 244
Kingdom of Wei, 262

**L**

Laozi, 28, 29, 36, 175, 177,

201, 226, 236, 237, 270
Le Guang, 266, 267
Li Hongyuan, 90
life plan, 182, 183
Liu Bei, 213
Liu Chiu-chieh, 145
Liu Xiangxiu, 131
Liu Yuxi, 15
Logitech, 100

**M**

Macau, 274, 276
Mahayana, 221
Maitreya, 222
Mao Zedong, 62
maximize performance, 21
McDonald's, 118
McGill, Archie, 21
Mencius, 218, 227, 257
Meng Huo, 243, 244, 246
mental fortitude, 203
Milutinovic, Bora, 248
Ming dynasty, 237
Mosilei, 119, 127-129

**N**

Nash Balance, 253
Nash, John, 252

NEC, 100
Neoglory Group, 155, 165
Neumann, John Von, 252
Ningbo, 49
non-separation, 217, 219, 221, 222, 229
nothingness, 266, 270, 271

## O

oracle bones, 30, 32-34
oriental beauty, 141
outer self, 24, 174-177

## P

Passion, 78, 93, 95, 97, 195-200, 203, 208, 209, 228, 238, 239, 264, 280
Peacebird Group, 49
Peters, Thomas J., 183
possibilities, 35, 45, 49, 53, 56, 60, 82, 120, 135, 143, 175, 196-198, 245, 247, 264, 266-269, 270-272
Prince Cao Cao, 262, 264
Prisoner's Dilemma, 252

## Q

Qian Zhongshu, 239

## R

Reasoner, Harry , 20
Red and Black Game, 4-6, 9
*Ren* Coaching Model, 8, 9, 30, 42, 43, 45, 49, 50, 89, 104, 134, 175, 177, 178, 181, 191, 192, 200, 222, 259, 280
responsibility, 47, 87, 91, 96, 97, 100, 101, 103, 104, 111, 128, 147, 148, 156, 186-190, 195, 198, 211, 213, 217-219, 222, 223, 225, 226, 233, 249, 264, 280

## S

Samsung, 42
SARS, 52-54, 60-62
Sartre, Jean-Paul, 202
Schultz, Howard, 179, 180
Seattle, 179, 180
self-examination, 96
selflessness, 158, 232, 237, 241

Senge, Peter, 183
Shanghai, 49, 86, 91, 151, 156, 158, 160, 161, 275, 277-279
Shanghai Media Group, 45
Shenzhen, 68, 70, 72, 131, 141, 154, 161, 211, 277, 278
*Shu*, 178, 179, 181, 182, 185, 200, 243, 244
SMEs, 165
Sony, 42, 100
Starbucks, 179, 180
Sun Yat-sen, 263
Sun Tzu, 228

# T

Taiwan, 27, 100, 107, 116, 154
Taiyuan, 83-86, 91
"Take a Letter to Garcia", 225
Tang Dynasty, 15, 27, 238
Tang Liqin, 67
Tao, 28, 169, 178-182, 189, 200, 201, 236, 237, 270
Taoism, 24, 28-31, 36, 237, 270
team-building activities, 139
*The Art of War*, 228

*The Fifth Discipline, The Art and Practice of the Learning Organization*, 183
*The Great Learning* , 171, 172
*The Inner Game of Tennis*, 20, 23
The Nine-Dot Game, 192-197
The Nine-Dot Leadership Model, 192, 195, 197, 198, 259, 263, 280
*The Spring and Autumn Annals*, 25
*The Tao and Its Power*, 270
Three Kingdoms, 213
Three Pillars, 173, 177, 181, 182
Tong Jie, 115
Toproot Electronics Co, 145
trust, 17, 47, 48, 72, 91, 125, 126, 133, 139, 143, 150, 186, 191, 196-198, 214, 215, 220, 226, 242-247, 249, 250, 264, 280
Two Aspects, 173, 174, 176, 177, 182

# U

unlocking potential, 21

# V

values, 54, 182-185, 189,
    200-204, 229, 232
Vantage Gas Appliance Stock
    Co., 51

# W

Waterman Jr., Robert H., 183
Wei Jianhua, 87, 89
Welch, Jack , 11, 14, 260
win-win, 7, 49, 91, 111,
    196-198, 251-253, 255,
    256-259, 262, 264, 279,
    280
World Health Organization
    (WHO), 52

# X

Xu Shen, 33
Xue Hui, 237

# Y

Yan, Jason, 45, 47
Yang Ming-kung, 100, 106
*Yin*, 177-182, 184, 200
Yiwu, 155, 156, 160, 161, 164,
    165
Yuan Zhen, 238
Yuewang Jewelry, 44, 46

# Z

zen, 23
*Zen in the Art of Archery*, 23
Zhang Ruimin, 152
Zhang Yi, 179
Zhejiang, 44, 156
Zhongshan, 52, 53, 254
Zhou Xiaoguang, 155
Zhuge Liang, 213, 215, 243,
    244, 246